Is The Income Tax System Legal?

A Guide to the Canadian Income Tax System

by

Dr. Paul Duarte

authorHOUSE®

AuthorHouse™
1663 Liberty Drive, Suite 200
Bloomington, IN 47403
www.authorhouse.com
Phone: 1-800-839-8640

This book is a work of non-fiction. Unless otherwise noted, the author and the publisher make no explicit guarantees as to the accuracy of the information contained in this book and in some cases, names of people and places have been altered to protect their privacy.

First published by AuthorHouse 6/11/2008

ISBN: 978-1-4343-7000-6 (sc)

Printed in the United States of America
Bloomington, Indiana

This book is printed on acid-free paper.

Acknowledgements

I would like to dedicate this book to all the hard working people of this great nation, and a special thanks to my friend Carla Cooper, who has helped in so many ways.

I also want to thank you, Dr. Andrea Paterson and Cyril Silva, for their inspiration and suggestions, and many others for their assistance, comments and feedback.

I also want to thank my publishers, Author Services Representative, Lisa Metcalf for helping walk me through the process of getting this book published.

I wish to thank you all, for I am a blessed man to have friends such as yourself.

Contents

Introduction ix

Chapter 1   Is the Income Tax System Legal? 1

Chapter 2   What do we need to do? 20

Chapter 3   Self-Employment 29

Chapter 4   Credits and Deductions 57

Chapter 5   Other Credits and Deductions 86

Conclusion   Deferring 98

References 101

Introduction

I have spent twelve years, advising, counseling and teaching people on the best way to get the most out of a tax return.

Some listen, some don't but the one thing most have in common is that, plainly they want nothing to do with the taxman, unless absolutely necessary.

I am happy to say, that most of our clients are still with us today and if you are one of them reading this book, we love you and want to thank you for your business, friendship and support.

Some of our clients have gone through hell and high water with CRA, but most have had it quite easy without incident and we thank God for that.

But either way, the experiences we shared together, have built strong friendships and relationships.

So for all, and people like yourself, we have created this small easy to read book, to help you along the way.

We have tried to stick to a very basic grammatical and easy to understand vocabulary, regardless of one's academic standing, because I believe that if a book is too complex or too hard to read, most people lose interest and out the window it goes, especially on the subject of taxes.

My goal is to reach as many people as I possibly can, and regardless of their love or hate for the taxman, have a practical piece of literature that can be used as a guide and perhaps as a awakening to some ideas that they may or may not have thought off or heard off before.

But how do I go about writing a book on taxes, without sounding repetitious or write something someone else has written before.

We read so many articles that instruct people how to maximize their returns, but surprisingly enough, not many in a book form.

The general idea is pretty much the same and they all say pretty much the same things in pretty much the same way.

If I stepped on some ones toes in the course of this book, I apologize, it is not intentional, and I will always try to give credit where credit is due. Our common goal though, or at least I would like to think, is to help one another and not profit from them. I am sure.

Many think of tax matters as boring and something to be avoided. Well, for the most part, that is probably true.

If anyone has ever tried to read the Income Tax Act, it truly is one of the biggest fifteen hundred pages or so, snoozer one could ever read. I myself must have fallen asleep at least once for every page.

Although most of us just use the Act as a reference manual anyway, it is good to be well informed.

The tax system is a very complex world indeed and it is becoming even more complex year by year as new laws and regulations are passed all the time, with each new election.

Sometimes conflicting the old ones creating loop holes in the system, such as the ones involving charities, in which CRA is working relentlessly to close all the time and rightfully so.

The act of goodwill should never be exploited. Sometimes such matters take years, to discover, investigate and correct.

To topple that, there are so many individuals out there trying to scam the "system", so much so, that CRA has become hardened and at times difficult to work with, sometimes forcing them to impose ridiculous penalties and inquiries, especially when they lack information, or suspect people of hiding something from them.

There is a tax court in existence where problems can be disputed, but a more immediate and accessible institute had to be created and that is a tax ombudsman (A private ruling body designed to mediate conflicts between the general public and CRA) to deal with issues that arise with almost everyone at one time or another.

This regulatory body from my understanding is supposed to be due for implementation sometime in 2008.

Really we can't blame CRA though. It is we, the public who by trying to avoid paying taxes all together or in trying to outsmart the system that brought it upon ourselves.

You know the old saying; one rotten apple will spoil the bushel and CRA can't always tell the rotten apples from the rest of the bushel.

It is like that with everything in life!

There will always be some who think they can outsmart or beat the system and the rest will pay for it when they get caught.

This book does not try to outsmart anyone or the institution, at least not intentionally. There are some provocative situations and some ideas which some would question. But everything in this book is well researched and taken right out of CRA documentation or the Income Tax Act.

The idea behind it is to apply rules and regulations that have been already in place, and try to utilize them to maximize our returns, so that we keep what is ours and pay CRA what is rightfully theirs.

Like the good book say's "Render therefore unto Caesar the things which are Caesar's; and unto God the things that are God's."

We believe in a fair market system, in a system where we the people have the voice and the choice in what is best for our country. We believe in democracy and not the other way around.

Politicians and Government officials are public servants of the people, elected into office by the people for the people.

But we also believe that when certain laws and statutes are passed without majority approval of most Canadians, we belief that it is our God given right to make you aware of their existence and how they came about and if needed to change for the needs of many and not the minorities of this country, as it so often happens.

We are **not** opposed to paying our fair share of taxes.

What we do oppose, is greed, injustice, and foul play.

True we cannot fix the ills of the world, but we can make others aware of them and perhaps by working together we can make it a little better place than we found it, for the generations that follow.

Chapter 1

Is the Income Tax System Legal?

How did Income Tax come about?

Our Canadian constitution is comprised of the B.N.A. act, also known as the British North American Act (1867) as well as Human Rights Act.

Contrary to popular belief that, Prime Minister Elliot Trudeau had changed the constitution during his term in office, it was not so.

What was changed was the addition of the Human Resources Act to our constitution.

The BNA Act was written in order to establish a base in which this country was to be governed.

All laws introduced by all levels of government, whether municipal, provincial or federal had to comply with the BNA Act.

Any law that did not or does not comply has to be considered unconstitutional and thereby disregarded as law.

The constitution was written and owned by the people, for the people of this great nation.

To better clarify this point here is a quote from Mr. Murray Gauvreau. Mr. Gauvreau is a Canadian, lobbyist speaking on the Canadian Tax System and his speeches such as this one may be found online for everyone to see.

Quote. "There are two specific sections of the B.N.A. Act that deal with the delegation of authority between the Federal and Provincial Governments, Sections 91 and 92 deal with authority for various types of taxation, who has authority to levy which taxes, and various other areas of jurisdiction.

The Act is very specific in its direction. The right to tax income, known as "direct" tax, was delegated to the provinces; and it was clearly indicated that any monies so raised must be raised provincially, and used for provincial purposes. The Federal Government was denied the right to levy income tax.

On October 3, 1950, the Supreme Court of Canada handed down a decision in the case involving the Lord Nelson Hotel of Halifax, Nova Scotia, against the Attorneys-General of Nova Scotia and Canada. The case involved the transfer of powers from the Provincial to the Federal Government, and was directly related to the income Tax Act. In a seven-judge unanimous decision, the highest court in our land ruled that power transfers couldn't legally take place.

The Federal Government was given until 1962 to remove itself from all such power-transfer agreements, including the Income tax business, and scrap the Income Tax Act..."

Plain and simple the Federal Government has no legal or constitutional right to engage in Income Tax Business or direct taxation.

Again quoting from Mr. Gauvreau,

"It is interesting to note that the same sections of the B.N.A. Act that disallow the Federal Government the right to collect income tax, did however provide for a means whereby the Federal Government could raise capital. Sections 91 (14, 15, 16, 20, and 29) give the Federal Government the authority, and the responsibility, for the control and issue of our currency, based upon the resources and wealth of the nation. They were given an unlimited supply of debt-free money with which to operate the country. All they had to do was print it. And they did just that for the first 46 years of our country. Then, some 46 years after the Confederation, in 1913, our parliamentarians were poorly advised in committing a grave injustice to future generations of Canadians by passing an amendment to the B.N.A. Act (without referendum!) commonly known as the Bank Act.

By this act, the Federal Government gave to the banking system the sole right to create the financial credit (in reality, the "money") of our nation. And for the last 79 or so, years, the private banking system has been exercising this monopolistic prerogative of creating and controlling the Canadian people's financial credit.

Well, banks don't work for free... they charge "interest."

They even charge interest to the Government. And interest can never be repaid; it just keeps adding up, and up, and up, until today our national debt alone is approaching $600 billion"

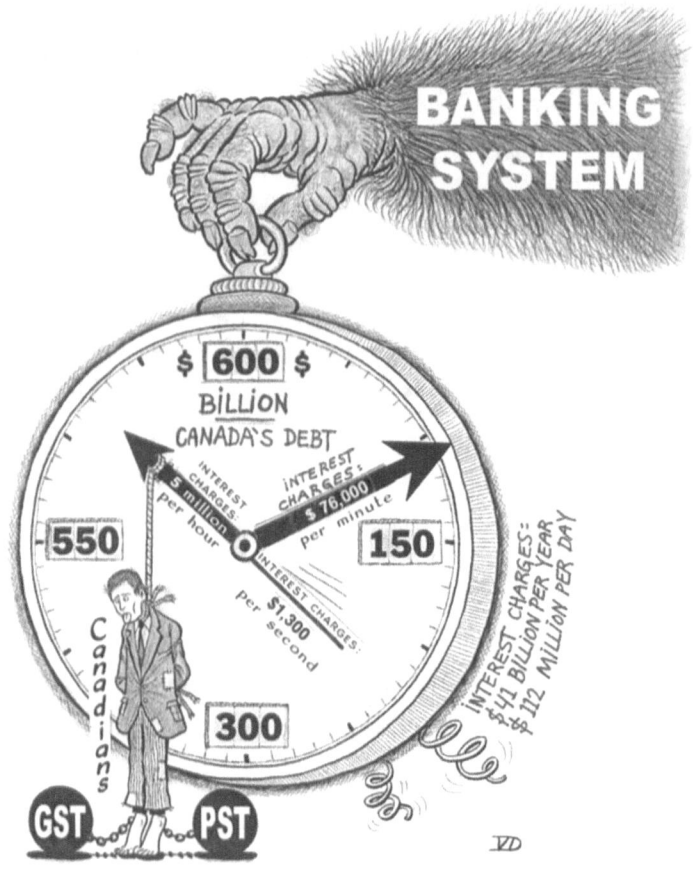

Illustration by Michael's Journal

Sections 91 and 92 of the BNA

91. It shall be lawful for the Queen, by and with the Advice and Consent of the Senate and House of Commons, to make Laws for the Peace, Order, and good Government of Canada, in relations to all Matters not coming within the Classes of Subjects by this Act assigned exclusively to the Legislatures of the Provinces; and for greater Certainty, but not so as to restrict the Generality of the forgoing Terms of this Section, it is hereby declared that (notwithstanding anything in this Act) the exclusive Legislative Authority of the Parliament of Canada extends to all Matters coming within the Classes of Subjects next hereinafter enumerated; that is to say, --

Exclusive Powers of the Parliament of Canada

1. The Public Debt and Property.
2. The Regulation of Trade and Commerce.
3. The raising of Money by any Mode or System of Taxation. (The raising of money through the System of Taxation such as indirect taxes, such as customs duties and excise taxes.)
4. The borrowing of Money on the Public Credit.
5. Postal Service.
6. The Census and Statistics.
7. Militia, Military and Naval Service, and Defense.
8. The fixing of and providing for the Salaries and Allowances of Civil and other Officers of the Government of Canada.
9. Beacons, Buoys, Lighthouses, and Sable Island.
10. Navigating and Shipping.
11. Quarantine and the Establishment and Maintenance of Marine Hospitals.
12. Sea Coast and Island Fisheries.
13. Ferries between a Province and any British or Foreign Country or between Two Provinces.
14. Currency or Coinage.
15. Banking, Incorporation of Banks, and the Issue of Paper Money.
16. Savings Banks.
17. Weights and Measures.
18. Bills of Exchange and Promissory Notes.

19. Interest.
20. Legal Tender.
21. Bankruptcy and Insolvency.
22. Patents of Invention and Discovery.
23. Copyrights.
24. Indians, and Lands reserved for the Indians.
25. Naturalization and Aliens.
26. Marriage and Divorce.
27. The Criminal Law, except the Constitution of Courts of Criminal Jurisdiction, but including the Procedure in Criminal Matters.
28. The Establishment, Maintenance, and Management of Penitentiaries.
29. Such Classes of Subjects as are expressly excepted in the Enumeration of the Classes of Subjects by this Act assigned exclusively to the Legislature of the Provinces.

And any Matter coming within any of the Classes of Subjects enumerated in this Section shall not be deemed to come within the Class of Matters of a local or private Nature comprised in the Enumeration of the Classes of Subjects by this Act assigned exclusively to the Legislatures of the Provinces.

Exclusive Powers of Provincial Legislatures

92. In each Province the Legislature may exclusively make Laws in relation to Matters coming within the Classes of Subjects next hereinafter enumerated, that is to say, --

1. The Amendment from Time to Time, notwithstanding anything in this Act, of the Constitution of the Provinces, except as regards the Office of Lieutenant Governor.
2. Direct Taxation within the Province in order to the raising of Revenue for Provincial Purposes.
3. The borrowing of Money on the sole Credit of the Province.
4. The Establishment and Tenure of Provincial Offices and the Appointment and Payment of Provincial Officers.
5. The Management and Sale of Public Lands belonging to the Province and of the Timber and Wood thereon.
6. The Establishment, Maintenance, and Management of Public and Reformatory Prisons in and for the Province.
7. The Establishment, Maintenance, and Management of Hospitals, Asylums, Charities, and Eleemosynary Institutions in the Province.
8. Shop, Saloon, Tavern, Auctioneer, and other Licenses in order to the raising of a Revenue for Provincial, Local, or Municipal Purposes.
9. Local Works and Undertakings other than such as are of the following Classes, --

    a. Lines of Steam or other Ships, Railways, Canals, Telegraphs, and other Works and Undertakings connecting the Province with any other or others of the Provinces, or extending beyond the Limits of the Province:
    b. Lines of Steam Ships between the Province and any British or Foreign Country:
    c. Such Works as, although wholly situate within the Province, are before or after their Execution

declared by the Parliament of Canada to be for the general Advantage of Two or more of the Provinces.

10. The Incorporation of Companies with Provincial Objects.
11. The Solemnization of Marriage in the Province.
12. Property and Civil Rights in the Province.
13. The Administration of Justice in the Province, including the Constitution, Maintenance, and Organization of Provincial Courts, both of Civil and of Criminal Jurisdiction, and including Procedure in Civil Matters in those Courts.
14. The Imposition of Punishment by Fine, Penalty, or Imprisonment for enforcing any Law of the Province made in relation to any Matter coming within any of the Classes of Subjects enumerated in this Section.
15. Generally all Matters of merely local or private Nature in the Province.

In a few words and the long run, it is we the people who become slaves to the credit system and by adding insult to injury; we are taxed to hilt on top of that.

In 1913 Colonel Edward Mandell House, an advisor to the US President Woodrow Wilson and a supporter of socialism, dreamed up by Karl Marx, introduced to the US federal government the 16th amendment, known as the "progressive Tax".

Shortly after that in 1917 the Canadian Federal Government, surpassed the Provincial Governments, and introduced our present Income tax Act which was suppose to be a temporary measure and disguised as a war relief effort during WWI, which was known at the time as the War Income Tax Act.

This Tax however was in essence a ploy to reduce the ever-growing national debt.

Furthermore it was to be implemented as a voluntary levy of about 10% of income, to those whose income surpassed $10,000 per year.

The average income for Canadians at that time was approximately $250 per year.

Since then, in spite of the best efforts of Canadians to keep this tax out of the system, the Federal Government has increased the tax rate to some of our higher income individuals who sometimes pay as high as 65% of their gross income.

They have also removed some of the lower limits, so that now everyone has to pay.

Here is the government's version of the War Income Tax Act, taken directly off the Government of Canada web site.

1917 – Income Tax: Financing War through Taxes

In 1917, with the Income War Tax Act, the Government of Canada introduced a temporary general tax on income. The tax applied to both personal and corporate income.

Military and related spending had climbed substantially as a result of the First World War.

By imposing a direct tax on income a type of taxation that had until then been the domain of the provinces the government planned to increase its revenues enough to help finance the war effort. Previously, the bulk of federal government revenues had been raised through indirect taxes, such as customs duties and excise taxes.

Canada's sources of revenue were not enough to cover the increased expenditures resulting from the First World War.

The federal government had already borrowed huge sums of money to finance the war effort and its related costs.

This led to high inflation and a national debt that grew fivefold over the course of the war.

High unemployment at the beginning of the war had turned into a shortage of workers by the time conscription was implemented in 1917.

Rising inflation soon led to unionization, strikes, and pressure from farmers and workers for the federal government to tax the wealthier segments of society more heavily and to nationalize banking and some other industries.

The poorer segments of society felt they had already sacrificed enough for the war effort.

Although the Constitution Act of 1867 gave the Government of Canada the authority to impose any kind of tax, it had never before tried levying a direct tax on income. Since the provinces were limited to the imposition of direct taxes only, some of them had already implemented their own provincial income taxes long before the First World War.

Debt incurred because of war and post-war expenses such as veterans' pensions necessitated the continuation of the income tax after the war ended.

The financial burden resulting from the Second World War also brought about changes in the administration of income tax under the Wartime Tax Agreements (1941).

Under those agreements, the provinces allowed the federal government to collect their income tax revenues for the duration of the war. In exchange, the provinces received payments from the federal government.

On January 1, 1949, the federal government ended the Income War Tax Act and introduced the Income Tax Act, making income tax a permanent source of revenue for the government. Today, personal and corporate income tax accounts for approximately 60% of federal budgetary revenues.

The federal government now collects personal income tax on behalf of all provinces and territories except Quebec, and then gives the provinces their share of the revenues collected. While the federal government also collects corporate taxes on behalf of some provinces, Quebec, Ontario and Alberta have their own corporate tax systems and collect their own corporate taxes.

Notice that this tax was supposed to be a temporary measure, but the tax was dragged from World War I until the Second World War.

They found that the tax was necessary to fund pensions such as veteran pension, but how about now is it still necessary? I think that more than 60 % of federal Revenues are more than enough to fund veterans' pensions, don't you?

An increasing number of Canadians are putting money away for retirement through the purchase of RRSP's, is there still a shortage of funds or just mismanagement of funds. And why are Canadians taxed on that money as well when it is cashed? Was that money not taxed when it was earned?

In 1941 the provincial government under the Wartime Tax Agreement which was designed to balance out provincial services between the richer provinces with the poor, by allowing the federal government to collect on corporate, personal and succession duties in exchange for a fixed amount of money.

But this notion had been around for a while.

Canada's poorer provinces were demanding that for years prior to the Second World War, but the war only precipitated this action. In other words, CRA used the war as a reason to implement the idea.

This agreement was then again amended between 1942 and 1947, again between 1952 and 1957, again 1957 and 1962 and lastly between 1962 and 1977.

We can go into details and economics on how this agreement was amended but it is suffice to say that the whole thing was just a glorified ploy to part Canadians out of their hard earned cash.

Remember that we mention earlier? All laws introduced by all levels of government, whether municipal, provincial or federal had to comply with the BNA Act.

Any law that did not or does not comply has to be considered unconstitutional and thereby disregarded as law.

In essence the provinces did not have the authority to enter into any such agreement.

Notice also, from the government article, that it mentions that the federal government collects these taxes on behalf of the provinces except Quebec? There my friends is the witty way in which they justified this agreement, "on behalf". In other words voluntarily did so. It seems that Quebec was the only province with their common sense in tact, and guess what, they survived.

They then gave the provinces their share of Revenue.

But wait a minute? Why collect the money in the form of taxation from its citizens of those provinces and then turn around and give it back to the province?

Why do the provinces not do that themselves in a uniformed way and be in direct compliance with the BNA (Act)? Are the provinces such bad managers that they cannot manage their own affairs?

Why you ask? Who ends up with the cash? The government right? Not the people in whose funds it came from in the first place.

Illustration by Michael's journal

Can one escape the taxman?

This is what this book is about. We are going to discuss issues that are known to some and unknown to most.

Let me clarify one thing right off the top. I am not suggesting that we avoid paying our fair share of taxes.

That is classified as tax evasion; it is illegal and carries a jail term for good measure for those who think that that they can get away with it.

Every year CRA lists a number of such individuals on their web site, as an example to all that take the time to actually read it.

To a lesser degree, CRA will also list some of the minor tax felonies, which sometimes are created by their own doing or make work program to insure someone's own job security and existence.

I speak from experience, my ex-company was once also listed in The Gazette (CRA's official online news letter) for failing to file a CT23 after repeatedly sending them letter after letter, telling them that the company in question had no longer been in existence for years and it was dormant prior to their threats of making the problem public.

There are many ways that we pay taxes and dues, such as through our store purchases, licenses, fines, education (whether you have kids or not) or land tax just to name a few.

Paying taxes however, is not necessarily a bad thing.

They are required and essential to the maintenance of our towns and cities and the quality of life that we enjoy today.

What is questionable is in the way we are taxed on and how the funds are distributed.

They would tax your smile if they could get away with it, so for Gods sake if you have gold fillings don't smile. You probably paid taxes on them anyway when you bought them and installed them.

We hear of all kinds of government scams, kickbacks, taxes being forgiven to foreign countries; politicians scamming the system and wasteful spending in the millions.

God forbid should anyone from the working class, otherwise owe CRA money or seem like they are trying to pull something off. They will be all over you like white on rice.

But as I mentioned in the introduction CRA can't be totally blamed for that.

In all fairness, there are so many scam artists out there trying to beat the system constantly, that CRA has no choice but to be tough on everyone.

But when they do target you, you are in for a ride. They will usually try to make you pay up within 30 days on a figure that is usually much higher than what they estimate you owe. Commonly in the ten's of thousand, when in actual fact, most of the time you owe much less or even they owe you.

This action will force you to act and not just sit idle and wait until they take it off your next years return.

The real pain in the butt is that it takes months and in some cases years to resolve.

In good management, lies the answer to our problem not only on a personal level but national as well.

Not by taxing ones hard earned income on a federal level, but efficiently using and not misusing funds from all other sources.

Some of the mistreatment or misdirected funds that we have just previously mentioned, if it were done by any one of us, they would throw you in jail and throw away the key for quite a long time.

However, when done on a government level, it is all good and well, wiped off the board only to start all over on a clean slate. We need not go far to know this is true, all one needs to do is turn on the tube and hear it for ourselves from time to time.

We could bring up so many specific cases and incidents that we read in the news in which almost everyone is aware, but that is not our purpose or issue to discuss them at this time.

Our real concern here and the concern of every Canadian reading this book is why we pay taxes on our hard earned dollars, on what I like to refer to, as sweat equity.

Or in a case just as discerning! Why our senior members pay taxes on RRSP's or RIFF's (Retirement Income Funds) when the purpose of that money is to relieve the financial burden of social assistance (such as CPP and OAS), in which supposedly comes from federal taxes collected over their working years to provide a decent living to our elders upon their golden years.

After all they have paid their dues, have they not? So why do they have to keep on paying taxes until the day they die?

We will be discussing this issue in detail as we move along.

There are many ways that we can retain what is rightfully ours.

Many of us hire professionals to find deductions on things we may not be aware off. In most cases this is a wise and prudent move.

For some of you clever lot, the tips in this book combined with your knowledge are enough to get you a great refund.

But it is our belief that there is nothing like being informed or just plain smart to get a refresher from time to time.

The GST

Goods and Services Tax is in my opinion another illegal measure of taxation. In Newfoundland / Labrador, New Bruinswick and Nova Scotia it is known as the HST (Harmonized Sales Tax).

The GST was designed to replace the 13.5% Manufacturers' Sales Tax (MST) and the Federal Telecommunications Tax of 11% in 1989, by the Progressive Conservative government under the leadership of Brian Mulroney to ease International competitiveness by manufacturers.

But guess who picked up the tab.

You guessed it. You and I, the end user! Or should I say the end loser.

If the responsibility of taxation falls on the shoulders of the Provincial Governments to implement taxes and those responsibilities are not transferable to any other sector of government in accordance to the BNA Act, then the GST too is illegal and unconstitutional.

Every business, either sole proprietor or otherwise, must register for a GST number if their total sales reach thirty thousand or more.

Anything below this mark, registering is purely voluntary except for taxi operators, which are mandatory to get a GST number regardless of their income.

However since it is here, you might as well know how to get some of it back.

If you are retailing or wholesaling and making $3,000 or $300,000 I encourage you to register anyway.

Here is why, as quoted directly from the CRA web site!

Registrants can claim a credit to recover the GST/HST that is paid or payable on purchases used to provide taxable goods and services. This credit is called an input tax credit and can be claimed for the GST/HST paid or payable for goods or services acquired or imported for use, consumption or supply in their commercial (taxable) activities.

GST/HST registrants who provide taxable goods or services have to charge and collect the GST or HST on their sales.

If the GST/HST collected is greater than the GST/HST paid or payable, the difference is sent to the CRA. (Registrants in Quebec send their payment to the ministère du Revenu du Québec.)

If the GST/HST collected is less than the GST/HST paid or payable, a refund can be claimed.

There will be months that you will no doubt have to pay in, even on a part time business.

But for the most part, unless you are running a real successful business, I am willing to bet that you will be owed more than you have to pay in GST and CRA will not volunteer to share that information with you, unless you are registered.

The amounts are usually small and considered negligible, but to the average Joe trying to make ends meet, it can make the difference between being short on the rent and having it paid on time.

Registering is free; it can usually be set up with one phone call.

The numbers are; English 1-800-959-8287, French 1-800-959-7775, Quebec 1-800-567-4692. You may also find these numbers in the blue pages of your local phone book or online in the CRA web site.

If this tax was to ease the competitiveness on the industrial and commercial sector doing business globally, who stands the most by profiting?

Is it each Canadian who will have the satisfaction of buying goods and services at a discount or cheaper?

Did the price of gas come down since the introduction of the GST?

Have the prices of anything come down since the GST?

Also do you think that any of that money has really ended up in the hands of those that it was intended for?

Yes perhaps in the hands of the private businesses and affiliates of those whom have orchestrated the tax in the first place, which in many cases are ran by their friends and/or relatives.

Better in your hands than theirs, I say!

Goods and services! What goods, what services?

Illustration by Michael's journal

Chapter 2

What do we need to do?

What do we need to do to keep what is legally ours.

Most of us work a forty hour a week job, some more, come home relax and get paid at the end of the week.

Your employer takes out approximately thirty percent (give or take) of your cheque in what is known as deductions.

After a hard weeks work, one sits on one's lazy boy or favorite chair with cheque in hand and says, "but…but…but, where did it all go and where is the rest all going"? Let's not forget that after deductions, you still have to pay a large chunk of it in taxes on everything else you purchase.

Well some of it is going for health care, the fire department, police services or to road repair. True enough!

Yes! That why you pay 14% taxes on all goods you buy, 35% plus on the fuel that goes in your car or lawn mower, sometimes ridiculous land taxes on property that is suppose to be yours in the first place?

(Which was taxed when you have already paid for on its purchase), on groceries, and the day-to-day things that we consume.

Isn't the government already generating millions from fines and impositions, such as licenses and registration fees that are suppose to be delegated for the same purpose?

So why pay taxes on your income as well?

To those of us who have a regular employment, your HR department at work should be taking enough money out of your cheque, so that you will end up getting you back a small refund at the end of the year.

But let's face reality, that thirty odd percent that you have been deducting every week, is for the most part gone out of your gross income. It is suppose to be delegated to your social assistance in which you are taxed on again as well later in life.

But wait! It does not have to be for good, at least not all of it, unless you let it be.

I don't think that a few people or this book for that matter, in speaking up against the injustices that have been imposed on us, and which have been ingrained into the taxation system, is ever going to change back the judicial clock and rectify the wrongs our government has created and implemented over the years.

It happens all the time, they think it, they impose it, and they pass it into law.

We vote them out off office on the next election, and the next one continues on the same tradition.

Ever ask yourself why? That is a subject for another time.

Now if you are content with the way our politicians do things, that is great and this material is not for you.

But if you are not! Then here are some things you need to do.

You need to find a way to claim part or nearly all of your expenses.

How do we do this? We do it buy using the law itself and the many loopholes that are created when a system becomes too complex.

To prove just how complex, try what I have done so many times. I called CRA personally for one reason or another, get advice from one person and on another day get contradictory advice from another!

Ok! Let's get to the point!

Always, file your tax return on time! Filing late or not filing at all will only attract undue attention to you.

Be honest! That too will only bring you undue attention and hassles you don't need, if you are not.

Never prepare your taxes by hand, invest in a good software program.

As a matter of fact if you file for a business GST, by law under the GST memoranda series, section 15.2, one is required to keep electronic records when filing their business GST for a period of 6 years.

There will always be something you might miss.

Preparing your taxes by hand, unless you are really good and un-forgetful, is like committing shopping lists to memory.

You always come home with one or two items short. And CRA will not voluntarily point it out what you have missed in most cases.

As far as their concerned, you are responsible for your own mistakes and in part they have a point.

Can you imagine CRA having to correct 20 or 25 million tax returns a year?

Perhaps you have heard of the 3 D's in tax planning, if have not, they are as follows:

Divide, Deduct and Defer, almost all tax planning fall within one or more of these categories.

One of the easiest ways to accomplish this and is accessible by anyone is to have a legitimate part time or full time business such as a home business.

Why a home based business?

A home-based business is probably the simplest and easiest type of business to operate.

The Canadian standard of living or living costs doubles every 14 years or so.

The average Canadian makes approximately $35 to $40,000 a year; about 60% of us make less than that, making it difficult to save for retirement or make ends meet for that matter.

Also the amounts of taxes we pay are not proportional to our incomes and still the retirement system is decaying.

So any additional income from a part time business or from your tax return is more than welcome by most of us.

A home-based business is something you do in the evenings, or the weekends or both, in addition to your present employment.

Selling illegal drugs does not count, that will only get your sorry butt in jail or dead.

Who knows, you may even make a success at it and change your career and your life, by doing something you love into a full time business.

There are literally hundreds of businesses ventures one can get into and start up.

The numbers of ventures are as diverse as people themselves.

From a cleaning business, lawn cutting service, mail order, a handyman service, small engine repair to a global Internet business reaching customers or clients from all corners of the globe. The options are endless!

However most of these, carry some sort of overhead, expenses and in some cases employees, education and a bit of expertise.

There are some risks as well, such as start up costs, tied up investments, sometimes taking years to recover, and government or health issues to deal with, who knows whatever else.

As a tax shelter, these businesses or any business, are just as good, but not without some aggravation, frustration and some constipation.

So that being said, my favorite of all business ventures has to be Networks.

Some of you will probably upon reading this will say, "Are you nuts? I have been in that non-sense before and it does not work.

But before you discard the idea and you are probably right, did you ever consider it from a tax point of view?

Some will close their minds to the mere suggestion, but we are not here to convince why it works or doesn't work, but how you can look at it in a different light to benefit you and protect you from having to pay in, in some cases, year after year.

After all some of these companies have had a bad wrap in the past.

For example, Amway a few years back.

The Canadian government accused them, of their Independent Business Owners (IBO's) not paying their fair share of taxes from the retail sales of the product, and in some cases that was probably true.

So they had to pay the government a nice sizable chunk of cash to account for all the taxes they figure it was owed to them, which is usually much higher than what it actually is.

I do not blame Amway in any way; I happen to think that Amway were and is a great and honorable company. Why should Amway have been responsible for their IBO's negligence?

The proper thing that should have been done is go after the negligent members and not the company itself.

But that! My friends would have been an almost impossible task and so going after the company itself would be much more lucrative and easy money.

This is like the laws they have on bartenders. Where a bartender can get charged or sued if someone leaves the bar drunk and kills someone while driving impaired.

Are bartenders babysitters? Where they have to be responsible for the irresponsible? No!

If you drive under the influence, grow up and take your own medicine if you're caught.

In order to keep this problem from happening again, Amway started to charge their IBO's taxes on the retail value of the product.

One would think that, that solution would be enough, but no!

Just recently on the news CRA is now harassing Avon, Quixtar (Amway's sister company) and Ebay, to find out if their members are really signed up for a legitimate reasons, or if they are in business just simply using it as a tax shelter.

They are targeting the biggest and the best, why? These companies are lucrative and if they have succeeded in suing them in the past, they will keep trying again and again.

Well that will be a difficult task for CRA wouldn't you say? Since some people do not sell to anyone except themselves, they will sponsor others who will do the selling for them and that is fine and legal as well.

So it does not matter if their IBO's retail or not for two reasons, (1) is that the retail taxes, **not wholesale**, has been paid at the source, and (2) even if they do not sell personally, their downline (as the people under them are called), do!

When will they ever be satisfied, and focus their efforts in more pressing matters.

Even if anyone, did get in a network for a tax shelter, the rich of our society who rarely pay taxes or very little, do it all the time.

The only difference between them and you is that they can afford expensive CA's (chartered accountants) and tax lawyers in which their fees become a write off as well, and you can't at least not initially.

But you may be thinking! Ok, but what they do, is it legal?

Absolutely! Everything they do and the way they do it, corresponds with the law.

They just happen to know how to manipulate the law to work in their favor. That is what this book is about, at least in part.

But please, DO NOT join any network simply as a tax shelter for the sole purpose of writing off all sorts of expenses against your other sources of income.

Even though what I teach in this book is all legal and above board, CRA will at some point check you out, if they do not see a reasonable expectation of profit.

Networking is one of the simplest forms of owning your own business. It is not hard, use the products you sell and get a few friends involved. The products will move themselves if everyone takes part in it. It's that simple.

You may not make a fortune, but it will benefit you in more ways than one, believe me.

And you might even have a bit of fun and meet new people in the process.

Why networks? Simple!

They are very inexpensive to join, usually under $300, duplicable so there is no direct competition, one is covered by the company umbrella, so that there is not need for vendor permits, licensing and registration (except to the network itself), little or no overhead and just about anyone can operate it from the comforts of one's own home.

A marketing system that is pretty much like a franchise, without the startup costs

This type of business will also give you the freedom and the time to spend with your family or involve them in your endeavor if you choose.

Especially if you already have a regular nine to five job, and evenings and weekends is the only time you have to spend with them.

There is nothing wrong with a Network as a home based business, provided that it is ethically, morally and fairly constructed.

The business structure is not poor; it is actually a very well organized way of doing business. It is only how we manage these businesses that makes them or breaks them.

There are literally hundreds of deductions in which you can apply to your return and unless you have a good understanding of tax law, you really should seek the advice of a tax professional.

At least you will be armed with some info, and not only will you be able to make suggestions to your bookkeeper, but also weed the good ones from the bad.

Take advantage of what applies to your particular situation, but here we are going to discuss only the most common issues that apply to almost anyone.

Chapter 3

Self-Employment

Why a network for a part time biz?

Thousands of business minded individuals use this strategy all the time. Here is why!

Networks are big business. Wall Street Journal reported a while back that 94% of client seekers used a form of networking or another to seek out new clients.

A network home business is perhaps one of the best ways to create tax deductions. Aside from the benefits previously discussed.

Networks offer an easy, trouble free, low cost, low maintenance way to earn an income and deduct your business expenses.

In addition to that, when you sign up, you automatically become a husband and wife team, which means that you have the option of writing off your expenses 50/50 or alone.

Sometimes one spouse wants to have a part time business, but the other has no interest in doing so.

In such case, you would claim the business solemnly 100 % by yourself.

But don't expect to make a great deal of money, or become rich on it, because the odds of that happening are fairly low.

Out of hundreds of thousands of Business Owners, only about 5% make enough money from it, to actually quit their jobs and become financially free.

Then again, perhaps you have what it takes to be one of those 5%.

You know, they say that 20% of the people control 80% of the world's wealth and 80% of the people the remainder 20% of the wealth.

For most of us we are not sales people or have a magnetic personality that attract people like flies to honey, so we have to be satisfied with being in that ninety five percent.

But on the other hand, when we share thoughts or ideas to another we are in a way selling that thought or idea. When we apply for a new job, we are selling ourselves, when we are courting or dating, again we are selling ourselves to our mates.

In a way, in almost everything we say and a great deal of what we do is selling, but yet we say that we are not sales people.

A moment to think about....

Let me give you an example, in a particular Network, which I am personally involved with, at least until they read this book (lol), all the products that are moved through you or your group.

There is a Business Value assigned to each item, which determines what one gets paid on. Usually less than what one would pay for the product itself, unless you order most items from their exclusive product line as opposed to mostly ordering brand name products.

The idea is to sponsor as many people into the network as possible and collect a small percentage from each active member of your group that reach a minimum number points per month.

These people could be your old college buddies, family members, friends of the family, professors, coaches, tutors, your boss, your bosses friends, club members, church members.... Whatever!

Great concept, the only problem is that it is difficult to convince someone that this is a good idea and even harder to get them motivated to purchase the products.

The fact is, that even though the products are of great quality, they are a bit expensive by comparison to most stores, and for most people, they are looking for cheap bargains not quality.

In all fairness though, you only get what you pay for, and the products are competitive with some of the upper class stores, society has to offer.

But here are some reasons on why the prices of these products are justified.

1. You have to spend your money on the products, whether you buy them from the store or from the Network. So it is money you are going to spend anyway.
2. The products are usually of the highest quality.
3. The tax savings are far greater than the cost of the products anyway.

It is a win, win situation, but that being said, after one signs up for a couple of months, most get discouraged, and either do nothing or quit.

Don't feel bad if you fall in that category though, because almost 95% of people who sign up for Networks quit within the first year, based on the cost of the product alone or just plainly don't understand or grasp the concept.

Ultimately, they will tell their friends that it is a waste of time, which only adds to the difficulty in sponsoring others who want to try and beat the odds.

But let's get back to the biz. By their own accord and business plan, one has to maintain a total Business Value, for a month, for the entire group including ones own consumption, of at least 37,172, which in reality is more like $45,000 or better per month in sales, every month, in product movement through your network, to make a bonus income of about $1,638.88 a month. Off course if you have a talent for retail those figures are much higher.

If you have been involved a number of years and one puts in a great effort into it, that number grows exponentially and you can achieve great wealth by doing it relentlessly, this is also a true fact.

If this is your goal, most companies and upline have great tools to make it happen for you, but as I said before, it requires great efforts, hard work, timing and a bit of luck.

Bottom line, unless you are prepared to build a huge network, (and some people have) moving tens of thousands every month you will not get rich very quickly. Nor do they claim that you will.

But here is a great tip. Any money that you do make in bonuses paid to you by the network, invest them in an RRSP and that bonus becomes another tax deduction on your return.

So that being said, you might not make a great deal of money from it, but you will, get back a great tax return for trying, by reducing the net income you earned from your job, at least until you turn a profit.

CRA knows that there is a reasonable expectation of making a profit; they also know that for the first 3 or 4 years most businesses barely recover what they have put into it. So a loss is not uncommon, but they do expect you to make a profit at some point and you can.

But how does one go about choosing a network? There are so many out there.

Simple really! Go for the biggest and the best with a great track record.

Here are some of the things to look for.

* Low start up cost with no quotas or inventory - This is a particular issue that gives networks a bad wrap.

    When a company or upline convinces people, that they need to keep inventory, or buy into a quota every month.

    Off course the pumped up individual, believes that the products will be moved in a matter of days or at least in a couple of weeks and when that does not happen, he or she is left with a room full of product that sits around forever until the poor chemo quits and ends up giving most of it away to his relatives for Christmas and birthdays.

    I stress the only inventory one should have in the home, if one chooses to do so, is the inventory that one consumes themselves.

    Otherwise it is a foolish notion to keep things that you will never use with the intentions of selling it to someone else, like 20 water filters, 50 brushes or half a dozen sets of luggage.

    What I mean by personal inventory is things that you will use up (consume) over a course of the month or less and only by choice, not motivated by someone else. Nothing more, nothing less!

The best way is to just purchase directly from the company, what you need when you need it.

If someone offers you a network scheme that involves quotas and or inventory, the best think to do is say "Thanks, but no thanks".

• A company that has not only a large diversity of products, not just one type of product, but just about everything under the sun. Their own brand names as well as common names that we all relate to, like Sony, Campbell, Proctor and Gamble and Panasonic. A company that does not limit themselves, but who has a large group of affiliates as well. Companies that work with them and pay you for using them. Like credit cards, hotel discounts, gas discounts, Cell phones, and so on.

• Consumables - It is important to be a part of a network that carries consumable products.

Consumable products generate sales month after month, such as vitamins, food items, toiletries, cleaning solutions and so on, product that one needs month after month no matter where one gets it from.

• Residual Income - Residual income is commissions, or better yet, royalties one gets paid from renewed business whether it is done by your own effort or the effort of others, such as a book or a movie or a song.

When a songwriter, writes a hit song, every time a record is sold he or she collects royalties from that   album   or CD year after year.

The same applies to Networking, every time a product is sold within your network one collects a   residual or royalty from whatever is sold, from people one may or may not even know.

So there is no need for one to be there or oversee day-to-day operations, especially if one falls ill or is away   for several months. The income keeps coming and does not decrease.

It is hard work from day one, but once a group or network is established, the need for maintenance is fairly low or none if the network picks up momentum and self perpetuates.

- A solid compensation plan - The best way to understand Network Marketing compensation plans is not to try to figure it out, even though their reference manuals explain it in detail, the best way may still be to actually speak to those who have been at it for a while.

  One can usually rub shoulders with these people at meetings and conventions or even by corresponding over e-mail.

  Don't get too hung up on the plan though, since this is not the focus of our discussion. But it is nice to get a bit of compensation for all the work one puts in, especially if that compensation comes in the form of a tax refund.

  Speaking to some of these people may or may not be a very accurate measure of their actual income,   depending on who one talks to because there are those who live beyond their means and inflate their status to make themselves look a little bit better than they are, but it still gives you an idea. I mean if the guy or gal is a millionaire by testimony of the company or colleagues, even if the stories are inflated, he or she is still a millionaire.

- No Billing or Collections - Get involved with a company where it is possible, where the customer does not have to go through you to order their product, but simple order it online using a number that you have provided them given to you by the company.

  That way, customers can order what they want, when they want, with or without your help.

- A solid track record - Get involved with a company that has been around for a while. If a company has been around since Moses was a toddler, chances are that this company is stable and knows the ins and outs of networking.

You want to be a part of a network, which has an unlimited amount of resources, and sell or get involved with almost anything one commonly uses.

"Be cautious thought as mentioned before DO NOT get involved with a company that one must maintain a quota, more often than non you end up spending more than you make, or companies that focuses on one product which will leave you with many things that could have been written off and one cannot due to their expensive inflexibility and lack of selection."

Why is this important? Well simply this.

When you become a part of the company, they assign you a membership number in which you become what they refer to as an Independent Business Owner (IBO).

So in essence even though, they encourage you not to look at it as a tax shelter, as with any business there are tax advantages that will greatly help your tax return and get a great refund.

They also encourage you, not to carry an inventory, and in reality you need not to. Unless one chooses to do so on their own accord!

But from a business point of view, everything you buy, everything you sell and everything you use or give away is part of an inventory, a personal inventory.

If one is considered an "Independent Business Owner" key word is being Independent.

Then everything you do, you do so, for your business at one's own discretion within the company's guidelines off course.

Dr. Paul Duarte

Here's the beauty of it all.

On your personal income tax return, you have something called Statement of Business Activities. Below is a sample on what this form looks like.

Canada Revenue Agency Agence du revenu du Canada	STATEMENT OF BUSINESS ACTIVITIES		2

For more information on how to complete this form, see the *Business and Professional Income* guide.

Identification

Your name		Your social insurance number	-	-

From:	Year	Month	Day	To:	Year	Month	Day	Was 2006 your last year of business?	Yes ☐	No ☐

Business name		Main product or service

Business address		Industry code (see the appendix in the *Business and Professional Income* guide)

City, province or territory	Postal code	Partnership filer identification number

Name and address of person or firm preparing this form	Tax shelter identification number

Business Number	Your percentage of the partnership	%

Income

Sales, commissions, or fees				a
Minus – Goods and services tax/harmonized sales tax (GST/HST) and provincial sales tax (if included in sales above)				
– Returns, allowances, and discounts (if included in sales above)				
Total of the above two lines			►	b
Net sales, commissions, or fees (line a minus line b)	8000			
Reserves deducted last year	8290			
Other income	8230			
Gross income (total of the above three lines) – Enter on the appropriate line of your income tax return	8299			c

Calculation of cost of goods sold (enter business part only)

Opening inventory (include raw materials, goods in process, and finished goods)	8300	
Purchases during the year (net of returns, allowances, and discounts)	8320	
Subcontracts	8360	
Direct wage costs	8340	
Other costs	8450	
Total of the above five lines		
Minus – Closing inventory (include raw materials, goods in process, and finished goods)	8500	
Cost of goods sold	8518	►	d
Gross profit (line c minus line d)	8519		e

Expenses (enter business part only)

Advertising	8521	
Bad debts	8590	
Business tax, fees, licences, dues, memberships, and subscriptions	8760	
Delivery, freight, and express	9275	
Fuel costs (except for motor vehicles)	9224	
Insurance	8690	
Interest	8710	
Maintenance and repairs	8960	
Management and administration fees	8871	
Meals and entertainment (allowable part only)	8523	
Motor vehicle expenses (not including CCA) (see Chart A on page 4)	9281	
Office expenses	8810	
Supplies	8811	
Legal, accounting, and other professional fees	8860	
Property taxes	9180	
Rent	8910	
Salaries, wages, and benefits (including employer's contributions)	9060	
Travel	9200	
Telephone and utilities	9220	
Other expenses	9270	
Subtotal		
Allowance on eligible capital property	9935	
Capital cost allowance (from Area A on page 3)	9936	
Total business expenses (total of the above three lines)	9368	►	f
Net income (loss) before adjustments (line e minus line f)	9369		

T2124 E (06) (Vous pouvez obtenir ce formulaire en français à www.arc.gc.ca ou au 1-800-959-3376.) Canada

38

Net income (loss) before adjustments (from line 9369 on page 1)		g
Your share of line g above		h
Minus – Other amounts deductible from your share of net partnership income (loss) from the chart below	9943	i
Net income (loss) after adjustments (line h **minus** line i)		j
Minus – Business-use-of-home expenses (from the chart below)	9945	
Your net income (loss) (line j **minus** line 9945) (enter on the appropriate line of your income tax return)	9946	

Other amounts deductible from your share of net partnership income (loss)
Claim expenses you incurred that were not included in the partnership statement of income and expenses, and for which the partnership did not reimburse you.

Total (enter this amount on line i above)

Calculation of business-use-of-home expenses

Heat	
Electricity	
Insurance	
Maintenance	
Mortgage interest	
Property taxes	
Other expenses	
Subtotal	
Minus – Personal use part	
Subtotal	
Plus – Capital cost allowance (business part only)	
– Amount carried forward from previous year	
Subtotal	1
Minus – Net income (loss) after adjustments (from line j above) – If negative, enter "0"	2
Business-use-of-home expenses available to carry forward (line 1 **minus** line 2) – If negative, enter "0"	
Allowable claim (the lesser of amounts 1 or 2 above) – Enter this amount on line 9945 above	

Details of other partners

Name and address	Share of net income or (loss) $	Percentage of partnership %
Name and address	Share of net income or (loss) $	Percentage of partnership %
Name and address	Share of net income or (loss) $	Percentage of partnership %

Details of equity

Total business liabilities	9931	
Drawings in 2006	9932	
Capital contributions in 2006	9933	

Dr. Paul Duarte

Area A – Calculation of capital cost allowance (CCA) claim

1 Class number	2 Undepreciated capital cost (UCC) at the start of the year	3 Cost of additions in the year (see Areas B and C below)	4 Proceeds of dispositions in the year (see Areas D and E below)	5 * UCC after additions and dispositions (col. 2 **plus** col. 3 **minus** col. 4)	6 Adjustment for current year additions (1/2 x (col. 3 **minus** col. 4)) If negative, enter "0"	7 Base amount for CCA (col. 5 **minus** col. 6)	8 Rate %	9 CCA for the year (col. 7 x col. 8 or an adjusted amount)	10 UCC at the end of the year (col. 5 **minus** col. 9)

Total CCA claim for the year (enter this amount, **minus** any personal part and any CCA for business-use-of-home expenses, on line 9936 on page 1**) [ ]

* If you have a negative amount in this column, add it to income as a recapture on line 8230, "Other income", on page 1. If no property is left in the class and there is a positive amount in the column, deduct the amount from income as a terminal loss on line 9270, "Other expenses", on page 1. Recapture and terminal loss do not apply to a class 10.1 property. For more information, read Chapter 4 of the *Business and Professional Income* guide.

** For information on the CCA for "Calculation of business-use-of-home expenses", read Chapter 4 – Special Situations in the *Business and Professional Income* guide.

Area B – Details of equipment additions in the year

1 Class number	2 Property details	3 Total cost	4 Personal part (if applicable)	5 Business part (column 3 minus column 4)

Total equipment additions in the year **9925** [ ]

Area C – Details of building additions in the year

1 Class number	2 Property details	3 Total cost	4 Personal part (if applicable)	5 Business part (column 3 minus column 4)

Total building additions in the year **9927** [ ]

Area D – Details of equipment dispositions in the year

1 Class number	2 Property details	3 Proceeds of disposition (should not be more than the capital cost)	4 Personal part (if applicable)	5 Business part (column 3 minus column 4)

Note: If you disposed of property from your business in the year, see Chapter 4 in the *Business and Professional Income* guide for information about your proceeds of disposition. Total equipment dispositions in the year **9926** [ ]

Area E – Details of building dispositions in the year

1 Class number	2 Property details	3 Proceeds of disposition (should not be more than the capital cost)	4 Personal part (if applicable)	5 Business part (column 3 minus column 4)

Note: If you disposed of property from your business in the year, see Chapter 4 in the *Business and Professional Income* guide for information about your proceeds of disposition. Total building dispositions in the year **9928** [ ]

Area F – Details of land additions and dispositions in the year

Total cost of all land additions in the year	**9923**	[ ]
Total proceeds from all land dispositions in the year	**9924**	[ ]

Note: You cannot claim capital cost allowance on land.

Chart A – Motor vehicle expenses

Enter the kilometres you drove in the tax year to earn business income	1
Enter the total kilometres you drove in the tax year	2
Fuel and oil	3
Interest (see Chart B below)	4
Insurance	5
Licence and registration	6
Maintenance and repairs	7
Leasing (see Chart C below)	8
Other expenses (please specify)	9
	10
Total motor vehicle expenses: Add lines 3 to 10	11

Business use part: $\left(\dfrac{\text{line 1}}{\text{line 2}} \right)$ × line 11 _____ = $ _____ 12

Business parking fees	13
Supplementary business insurance	14
Add lines 12, 13, and 14	15

Allowable motor vehicle expenses: Enter the amount from line 15 at line 9281 on page 1

Note: You can claim CCA on motor vehicles in Area A on page 3.

Chart B – Available interest expense for passenger vehicles

Total interest payable (accrual method) or paid (cash method) in the fiscal period _____ A

$ _____ * × the number of days in the fiscal period for which interest was payable (accrual method) or paid (cash method) _____ B

Available interest expense: amount A or B, whichever is less (enter this amount on line 4 of Chart A) $ _____

* For passenger vehicles bought: • from September 1, 1989 to December 31, 1996, and from 2001 to 2006, use **$10**
• from 1997 to 2000, use **$8.33**

Chart C – Eligible leasing costs for passenger vehicles

Total lease charges incurred in your 2006 fiscal period for the vehicle	1
Total lease payments deducted before your 2006 fiscal period for the vehicle	2
Total number of days the vehicle was leased in your 2006 and previous fiscal periods	3
Manufacturer's list price	4

The amount on line 4 or ($35,294 * + GST and PST, or HST on $35,294), whichever is more

$ _____ × 85% = _____ 5

[($800 * + GST and PST, or HST on $800) × line 3] ▸ _____ − line 2: _____ = _____ 6
   30

[($30,000 * + GST and PST, or HST on $30,000) × line 1] _____ = _____ 7
   line 5

Eligible leasing cost: line 6 or 7, whichever is less _____ $ _____

(Enter this amount on line 8 of Chart A above)

* If you entered into a lease agreement before January 1, 2001, make the following changes to the chart:

	After 1990 and before 1997	1997	1998 and 1999	2000
• for line 5, replace $35,294 with:	$28,235	$29,412	$30,588	$31,765
• for line 6, replace $800 with:	650	550	650	700
• for line 7, replace $30,000 with:	24,000	25,000	26,000	27,000

Printed in Canada

In this statement you have a line entitled 'purchases during the year' (line 8320).

All of your purchases during the year go in there. This is your inventory purchase throughout the year.

You also have a line entitled Opening Inventory (line 8300) and all inventory that is still sitting on the shelf the year you do your tax return go there.

Minus what you have sold to anyone and what you have consumed. That goes in line (a) under sales and commissions.

That include groceries, cosmetics, vitamins and supplements, clothing or just about anything you buy from the network, which in this case is your supplier, that is to say your entire inventory.

However when it comes to your own consumption, there is no law that say's that you cannot sell them to yourself, your brother, your sister, your cousin or any other family member for higher or a lower price than you paid for it. This is totally your discretion

What you have just done and right off the top is created a tax credit, a deficit if you will on whatever you have purchased. After all it is yours, paid and bought for by your business.

For example, let us say that throughout the course of a year, you have purchased $5,000.00 in merchandise for your own inventory.

Out of that $5,000.00 you sold $2,000.00 to your customer base.

That $2,000.00 you will have to declare in line (a) as Income.

The remaining $3,000.00 you consumed it, but before doing so here is another tax saving tip.

Sell it to your spouse if he or she does not want to be part of your business or a family member and again if he or she is not part of your network, at a discount and let us assume that you have chosen to sell it for $500.00 dollars.

You claim that $500.00 as income unless you gave it away for nothing, but now you have to claim $2,500.00 as sales.

Well you have just lost $2,500.00 on this deal haven't you?

Be honest now! One might say, "But there is a tax liability on what you have consumed or gave away".

The fact is that we are being honest, since most networks in this country have already charged you taxes on the <u>retail value</u> at the source.

You are actually paying more taxes than you should on the product, but because the company (network) has no idea what you do with the merchandise once it is bought, this simple action protects not only the network in which you bought it from, but **you have also <u>paid to CRA the taxes due</u> on the products that you have purchased initially.**

Since CRA has already gotten their share of both taxes GST and PST, when you have purchased the product, whatever you do with it is your business, and the tax liability has been paid for. Even if you consume it, you have paid the taxes at the retail level of the product.

This act is also a safe guard, to prevent people from taking advantage of the system and not pay their retail tax obligation to CRA.

So you see, there is nothing illegal or unethical when the tax obligation has been taken care of at the source.

If you wish to get back the taxes on the personally consumed products, you will then have to file an adjustment form, provided by the companies themselves.

One can look at this as owning a restaurant, and you have your family members, business acquaintances, and friends drop in day after day and eat for free.

You still have to pay the cooks, the utilities, the food, the waitresses and the rent, regardless of how many people or how often they take advantage of your generosity, correct?

What do you do with the expenses that come out of your pocket as a loss? You right them off, right! This business or any other you decide to get into is exactly the same!

Now in addition to writing off what you sell at a loss from your own supply that could have been sold to generate income in the first place.

One may also claim any inventory that was carried over into the following year.

Remember that all tax liabilities have been paid for at the source, when the network charges you taxes on the retail value of the product.

If you own something other than a network, there are other deduction in this section of your return that one can take advantage off as well, such as direct wages, subcontracts and other costs of doing business.

You can write off a number of other expenses that come with running your particular business.

Here are some examples of the most common deductions or carrying charges that one can write off, no matter what type of business you're into (refer to example above).

Advertising: This type of expense is pretty much explanatory. It involves any kind of advertising, such as 100% of the cost of producing flyers, banners, and a Canadian newspaper, radio ads or televisions ads.

One can also deduct any finder's fees that come with advertising. One thing one has to keep in mind is that the gas and meals involving doing the footwork is also deductible elsewhere in which we will be discussing in a later subtitle.

Bad debts: These expenses are debts that you have incurred from bad business planning or monies you might have lend out from your business but was never recovered, in other words your accounts receivables.

For example, you make a deal with a customer to pay within a certain time, and the customer defaults on that deal and owes you the money at the end of your fiscal year.

You can choose to write that off as a bad debt to your company with interest.

However if the money is recovered the following year, that money has to be claimed as income in that year and off course taxed as such.

Business tax, Fees, Licenses, Dues and Memberships: In this category, there are things that you can and some that you can't write off depending on the type of business that you are running.

Let's examine one issue at a time.

Business taxes - only applies if you have an office, or some other type of building in which you are charged a tax to run your business in that location by the landlord.

Fees – This is any kind of fee that comes with running a business such as if one is a tennis instructor or some other kind a coach and has to pay a fee for the use of a premises (club fees).

Basically any type of fee in which you are obliged to pay in the process of running your business.

License – This expense is a mandatory expense such as for example, a mechanic or any other professional who is bound by a license to practice his or her trade, usually yearly, but for some occupations once every few years.

This however does not include your driver's license since that is a motor vehicle expense and come under a different section of your return if you are using your car for business purposes.

Dues – Are relatively close to fees and are paid on a more regular basis, such as a union due, however once again union dues are written off in a different part of your return.

Usually with your T – Slips information.

Memberships – This is one that applies to all of those who are in any network. One can claim their membership and renewal fees. But on the same token, it also applies to anyone who is a member of an association, such as accountants, doctors, ministers and an array of other organizations to whom give credit and prestige to those belonging to them.

Delivery charges: These involve any expenses due to shipping merchandise, no matter what business you're in. These can be the post office, couriers, private companies or even if you ship merchandise by taxi. Any kind of cost involving sending and receiving goods.

The next few apply only to those who run a business outside their home office and do not necessarily apply to someone running their business from home. But I will list them just the same. One never knows, some of you may decide to run your part time business from somewhere outside the home.

These include:

Fuel - Such as heating oil and gas for lift trucks and generators.

Insurance – Such as a building, inventory or machinery.

Interest paid on the lease and on monies borrowed. Any money borrowed for legitimate business purposes.

Maintenance and Repair – On buildings and equipment.

Management and Administration – The cost of running that business.

Meals and Entertainment (Business Related): This is the cost of doing business over lunch meetings, dinner meetings and meetings over coffee.

You are entitled to claim fifty per cent off this deduction. Keep in mind that these also included monies spent such as promotional banquets, conventions and company functions where food and entertainment is a part of doing business even if it is just taking new prospects or clients for a drink, provided that it is part of conducting your business.

Unfortunately for some of you, your personal liquor or beer receipts are not tax deductible.

This deduction does only apply to businesses that regularly provide food, beverages, or entertainment to customers for compensation (for example, a restaurant, hotel, or motel).

A percentage of your car expenses: When one uses their car for business purposes, it is no longer considered a luxury, but a deductible necessity. The total amount cannot be deducted as one only uses the car a percentage of the time to carry on his or her business interests, but assuming one uses the vehicle say 30 or 40 % of the time, then one can deduct 30 or 40 % of all expenses affiliated with that vehicle.

Please keep in mind that is vital to keep all receipts, so if CRA requests them, you can prove those expenses. Car expenses have to be broken down in sections, because CRA does want to see in what manner one spends their money when it comes to car expenses.

Let's start with what percentage of car expenses can be used for business.

For the most part CRA requires that you keep a log with the mileage that you incurred while making an income from your business. However, they know that most of us are pretty sloppy in this area and do not keep a log.

What to do, what to do. The next best thing is estimating what percentage of your use of the vehicle, you spend working the business.

Even though CRA does not really condone this practice, most of the time they will accept this form of measure, unless you are being audit.

In which case if you do not have a log, they will guesstimate, what that figure should be and you will have to live with that.

Fuel – The average consumption of gas one used to conduct their business.

Interest – This only applies if you have leased a vehicle or financed your car in the year in which it was bought.

Insurance – The necessary evil in which one is enforced by law to have on his or her vehicle on the road.

Maintenance and Repairs - Again pretty self-explanatory.

Leasing costs – The cost of leasing your vehicle.

Parking and last but not least CCA (Capital Cost Allowance) – Capital Cost Allowance is the cost of depreciation on your vehicle.

You may claim depreciation on a vehicle that you own, but not on a leased vehicle since the car does not belong to you in the first place.

In most cases the vehicle is simply replaced by a newer model upon expiry of its contract.

Office expenses and supplies: Office expenses and supplies, even though listed in two different categories, in my opinion should be listed as one of the same, because there are not much difference's between the two.

These include Pens, pencils, paper, software and ink for the printer, but not computers, fax machines and other electronic gadgets. These get written off in the CCA (Capitol Cost Allowance) part of your return since these are depreciable items.

A few other things that you may not thought off, such as cleaning supplies for the office, water and water coolers, microwave even coffee and biscuits if you use these things to make your customers feel more comfortable (supplies).

All of which you can buy from your own personal inventory.

Legal and accounting fees: This is one of my favorites, since taxes and bookkeeping is my living.

This is any expense that involves representation, counseling or bookkeeping of your company.

Expenses such incorporation of your company, lawyer's fee that represent you in case one gets themselves into legal hot water regarding your business or to appeal a tax decision by CRA.

Property Taxes: Although property taxes show up in two different places in your Statement of Business Activities, if you are running your business from home, the only place you may claim the property tax besides the ON 479 is on the business-use-of-home-expenses, which we will talk about, a bit later.

This particular section on line 9180 refers solemnly to taxes on a building outside of the home, in which one has paid property tax on.

Rent: Even though this expense applies to buildings outside the home. However, you can claim rent in the Home Office section of this statement.

Salaries, wages and benefits - is another expense that does not apply to a home business, unless you have employees, even though you work from home.

Try to refrain from employing people on salary or wage. Hired them under contract, this way your employees will be responsible for their own tax liabilities.

Since they are self employed workers, they will have the opportunity to write of their expenses as well, as a cost of earning an income and it is also deductible for you since their income becomes a liability to your business.

As a self-employed worker, they would also have to take their own responsibility for things like workman's compensation, union dues and benefits.

Travel: There are basically three types of travel. There is personal, which is usually a vacation and this form of travel is not tax deductible. Unless one conducts business while on vacation, in which case, becomes partially business and partially personal.

Most people in Networks take advantage of type of travel, since one of the benefits of the business is to conduct it worldwide.

If these expenses are put on a credit it card, the interest on the business portion of the trip is deductible as well.

Some networks even have travel discounts for staying at specific affiliated hotels.

Due to the fact that most networks businesses can be conducted from anywhere in the world that has Internet access.

This form of travel is tax deductible, but only the business part of it. Such as meals, hotels and a portion of the Air, bus or ship fares, (approximately fifty per cent).

If one travels via a motor coach or motor home to conduct meetings all over the country the expenses related to that motor is also deductible as well as the interest on that vehicle.

The third form is purely business such as company-sponsored trips, conventions and meetings with clients.

In this case the whole trip is a hundred per cent deductible.

Telephone and Utilities: These expenses are deductible, but only the business part as well. In other words, if one uses the home phone for business, one can deduct the approximate time spent on the phone conducting his or her business and claim that portion on the return.

If you are in the financial position to do so, the best thing to do is have a separate line for your business or just use the cell phone and deduct all it.

Utilities however should be claimed in your home office expenses, unless you work outside of your home.

What can you claim from your business-use-of-home?

The amount you can claim is limited to the net profit of your business and even then, only a percentage of the area that you conduct your business in relation to the area of the whole house or apartment.

If you have a loss, or your home office expenses exceed your net profit, you may carry the unused portion into future years.

One may not however use in-home-business expenses to reduce your net income from your primary source of income that is usually your full time job.

One may also claim home office expenses as long as one can allocate that the space being used is part of their employment contract and the expenditures are used in direct relation to work activities and the employer is not reimbursing you for those expenses.

To deduct work expenses in relation to earn a living while employed by someone else, one needs to fill out a T2220 certifying that these expenses are indeed under the employment contract and submitted with your return to CRA.

If one is on commission, one can usually deduct a bit more.

Here are a few examples:

If you conduct any kind of work or meetings in your house, you may claim your TV and DVD player if you are showing training videos or material relevant to your particular business.

You may deduct interest on the mortgage provided you have one, property taxes, electricity, gas or oil, insurance, maintenance and part of the phone bill.

You may be able to deduct these expenses in proportion to the office space being used to the square footage of the house.

But! This deduction thing can get even more interesting.

What if you own a second business, or even a third or a Church Ministry?

Well! You can use some of the products from your network, sell them to your second business and write off the products from your inventory as supplies to the second business.

Suppose you own a second business, let us say a cleaning business.

You purchase cleaning supplies from the network, sell them to the second business and write them off as supplies in that second business.

This is known as leveraging. Or in the case where you have a ministry for example; you donate the supplies needed for the church as gifts in kind (donations).

Write off what you donate at their fair market value. In this case it would be the retail value of the merchandise (the church will need to issue you a receipt for the products though) provided that the church is registered as charity (read the section on charities in the CRA web site to find out more).

Before we go any further though, let me define what the government refers to as the Fair Market Value from their own literature, so that there is no confusion or misunderstanding.

Fair Market Value:

Quote "generally means the highest price that a property would bring, expressed in dollars, in an open and unrestricted market, between a willing buyer and a willing seller who are both knowledgeable, informed, and prudent, and are acting independently of each other.

Fair market value does not include any amounts paid or payable to other parties, such as commissions to sales agents or sales taxes like goods and services tax/harmonized sales tax (GST/HST) or provincial sales taxes".

In the case where one donates or sells to one self, you have become both the buyer and the sellers. But the wholesale and retail prices on the merchandise were pre-designated by someone else or in this case by a company.

But how about if you are employed by someone else and that someone owns a business such as a restaurant, a garage, a building, a store or whatever else.

Well, if you are in good league with the boss, perhaps he or she may even purchase the supplies from your personal or commercial sector of the business and allow you to make a second income outside your work duties.

If you are getting your work done and the employer cares about the welfare of his people, without having to dish out extra cash, on a raise, I am sure most employers would not have a problem helping you in that department. Thereby helping you get a great return in the process.

It may or may not make a big impact on your return, but it will generate a profit for you from the continuing sales and the bonuses your network pays you.

Another great way that one may profit from owning a part time business is that one is able to hire one's partner (usually the wife or husband) and split your income so as to lower your own income to a point where the tax liability if any becomes much smaller. We will be discussing income splitting a bit further down in a subsequent chapter.

What if one is already self-employed?

If one is already self-employed full time, getting a second business is also not a bad idea either.

Many of the world's success stories have second or even multiple businesses as tax shelters.

When you purchase anything from your network and sell it to your second business for whatever price you feel is a right (remember the tax liability has been paid at the retail level). You create a tax shelter from one of the two.

For example; you have a successful restaurant, and normally you purchase let's say disinfectant, dishwashing soap, coffee, toilet paper or just about anything that your second business sells.

You might normally pay $20.00 for a jug or can from your regular supplier.

But now you are part of this network that sells the same product, perhaps of better quality, perhaps not, but still it costs you $25.00 lets say, instead of your usual twenty.

But the thing is that you have purchased the product from the Network for your personal inventory for $25.00 when you normally buy it for $20.00 from your regular supplier!

Bummer! Right? Wrong! Why? Because you are turning around and selling the product to your restaurant for a dollar, that's why.

Well, one can say and cannot debate that a fair discounted value for this product is $20.00. Or cheaper by a different source, but everything is relevant and an item is only worth as much as someone else is willing to pay for it and in this case, you are only prepared to buy it from yourself at the price.

Therefore in the long run, you paid a dollar and you have created a tax credit of $24.00 on your first business.

On top of that, you have made a bit more cash from the bonus your network company pays you at the end of the month, which will cover for any delivery charges that you are probably already paying for anyway.

None of these practices are illegal or unethical you are only getting back the taxes you paid into it in the first place on a select few items, you are still paying business tax (which to me is still a mystery why), taxes on fuel, taxes on heat, hydro, water, sewage, at the source and the list go on. You have two companies; you buy from one and sell to another, plain and simple.

Once bought from the first company, the product is yours; the taxes on the retail value has been paid, so CRA got their money and should be happy, then resell it, give it away or throw it to the wind. The item is yours, you own it.

Chapter 4

Credits and Deductions

Income Splitting

The goal to income splitting is to shift income from a higher income earner to a family member with a lower income that is in a lower tax bracket.

Most commonly it is done between a husband and wife, but it can also be done between parents and children.

As of the year 2000 it is discouraged to do this with children under 18 as they are subject to a special tax and thereby eligible for a deduction.

In most cases your next of kin get paid as subcontractors to the business, not in the form of an allowance, but in a form of a wage or salary.

Assuming a fully employed husband / wife situation, where the husband is at a higher income bracket than his wife.

In many situations it may happen, that the scenario is reversed.

But for the sake of simplicity let us go with this example.

The higher income individual should use his income to pay all expenses including such things as paying off loans or outstanding taxes and provide funds to both his and her RRSP's.

While the lower income individual uses her income to save and invest.

Maintaining separate accounts is important so that if CRA questions the sources of income, it will be easy to establish.

RRSP's can also be used to split income during retirement years.

It is optimal that both partners have approximately the same value in RRSP's, however if one spouse has a pension but the other does not, it is important that the spouse without a pension has a much larger RRSP to balance their income during the retirement years.

Another way is to take advantage of this strategy is to apply to the Canada / Quebec Pension Plan.

Where only one spouse is entitled to retirement benefits or if one's benefit is much higher, then they can apply to this plan where they pool their money and 50% gets paid to one and 50% to the other, thereby putting more funds in the lower tax bracket individual.

Canada Savings Bonds in a child's name is not a bad idea either; however there is a wrong way and a right way.

The down side is that, usually the contributor usually pays the tax on the interest if the child is under 18.

The upside is that this does not have to be, if the contributor of a family that receives a Child Tax Benefit deposits this money into an account with the child's name, the interest is taxable to the child and provided that, that the child has no other income; the interest earned is tax-free.

Allow me to quote an example I read on the net right out of MSN money, which by the way is a great publication available to anyone who owns a computer with Internet access.

Quote "If your eight year old son earns $1,000.00 per year on a paper route.

This allows him to put $180.00 into an RRSP the following year.

Since his income is too low to be taxable, he won't be able to use the deduction immediately, but he can file the receipt and use the deduction in a future year, when his income is higher.

Repeating this over a period of, say, ten years, would give him a $1,800.00 deduction to reduce tax in his first year of full time employment.

Assuming his contributions were invested in a Canada Savings Bond at current rates, he would start his working life with over $2,000.00 in his RRSP.

By retirement this money could grow to be close to $50,000.

The only thing is that he must file a tax return to establish the right to the contribution room".

Interest and dividend income is attributed to the donor; this is not the case with capitol gains.

If an investment is made in an equity mutual fund as in an (RESP) Registered Education Savings Plan, registered as in a trust in order that one maintains control on the investment.

The capitol gains as well as the gains of the units sold, becomes taxable to the child.

Last but not least, my favorite. If a parent or a spouse owns a business,

They can hire his or her next of kin to work in the business, from doing the smallest task to the more complex in according to his or her ability.

The salary off course has to be within reason after all you cannot pay someone more than the company can afford.

A salary is a deductible business expense and allows children to build up a tax-free income as long as that salary does not exceed the basic amount, which also creates an RRSP contribution room, by which there, is no age limit for contribution. Just as long the child has an earned income.

RRSP's

Why invest in an RRSP?

Many of our seniors are faced with the burden of having to pay taxes on their RRIF's (Registered Retirement Income Funds) upon retirement or on survivor benefits.

We will touch upon those at the end of this chapter.

The government will tell you that they are giving you a break by allowing you to use your RRSP's contribution as a tax credit in the years that you are allowed to contribute.

But, are they really? Whose money was it to begin with? Yours right?

Money that you have earned and have been taxed on from the moment that you have earned it, right?

So who is doing whom a favor? You are putting that money aside to relieve the burden of social assistance, which the government will eventually claw back and already is doing so, on the more well to do citizens of our country.

You need proof? Here is a memo from CRA word for word to one of my clients.

But before we go further let me acquaint you on the difference between a deduction and a tax credit.

A tax deduction - is calculated on your income before tax. The higher your tax bracket, the more expenses you need to counter act your taxable income.

A Tax Credit – is worth the same regardless of your income or tax bracket. For example a $100, $500 or $1000 tax credit will reduce your tax bill by the same amount, regardless of what your income is.

Quote:

"Old Age Security Deductions for Higher Income Seniors

Under Canada's public pension System, seniors with an expected net income of more than $63,511.00 in 2007 tax year have to pay back all or part of their Old Age Security (OAS) pension.

We will be recovering these benefits each month as a deduction from your OAS pension.

Your deduction amount is calculated by Canada Revenue Agency (CRA).

They calculated your deduction based on the income you reported on your 2006 tax return.

Your deduction will start in the month shown in Box 1 and will continue until June 2008.

This monthly rate deduction can change if your income changes. If this occurs, we will send you another letter to let you know the new amount of your deduction.

If the amount in Box 3 is $00.00, it is because the CRA has advised us to stop the OAS deduction" unquote.

Perhaps someday they will even get rid of it all together, at least in certain sects.

So in reality they really should give you a tax break, not because the government is so loving and generous, but because in the long run it is the government who benefits by it all.

The more you put away for your retirement, the more Income Tax money, designated for social assistance, the government gets to keep.

Investing your money in an RRSP is one of the most important things that anyone can do, though. In spite of it all, it will insure security in your golden years if properly managed.

Perhaps even more so than life insurance, even though that insurance is an important and necessary part of ones portfolio, unless off course one has accumulated enough wealth that RRPS or insurance is not necessary.

But on the same token why would one not make their money work, instead of just leaving it sitting in a bank account losing interest.

Do not hesitate to max out your contribution room, if you can afford to do so, do it now.

Here is the reason why.

If you delay in investing your maximum contribution room, for whatever the reason may be. The difference between what you have invested and your contribution room could be earning hard earned interest, instead of sitting in your bank account earning nothing.

If let us say you delay by a few years, whether your investments are earning 5% or 10% that can reflect into several thousands of dollars that you have missed out on.

One may say that it is no big deal; one can just dump the whole amount in one shot. But it is a big deal; some of that money that you could have been earning will be lost forever.

If you know anything about dollar cost averaging and leverage, which we will not be getting into at this time, you will understand what I am talking about. But if you don't you will just have to take my word for it.

When it comes to RRSP's there is no time like the present.

Look at the RRSP contribution room that comes attached to your Notice of Assessment as something to be paid and not an option. This will benefit you 10 fold in the long run.

Off course some of us do not have the financial means of achieving that, but if you do, don't delay.

Most of the wealth community knows the benefits of investments, so we have no need to go there.

This book is guided toward the working class whom saving money is an important factor in their lives and a great necessity.

Interestingly enough, many people are still in the dark about RRSP's.

Ah! But wait, for those of us who cannot fill that contribution room there is another solution.

If you have ever put money aside for RRSP's before, you probably already know how to maximize it.

But we can go over it for those of you who do not.

It is quite simple really, like everything else in life, once you know how, after that it is a walk in the park.

The first thing you need to do is to have your taxes done about a week before the RRSP deadline.

DO NOT file it, but have it prepared.

Once you know what you are getting back on your return, borrow from your bank or any other financial institution that lends out RRSP loans.

A good number is usually about two thirds or there about, of what you're getting back.

Why two thirds? Because that percentage will allow you some space for contingency in case you do not get back the whole amount that you were expecting in your refund.

The expected tax credit is normally give or take about a third of amount invested, so if you invest $3,000 you will get back a tax credit of about a $1,000 or so.

Now invest that extra money back into the RRSP.

But wait! Now you have that big bill coming from the loan company in about thirty days. Right!

So in order to avoid paying interest on your loan, you file your return as soon as you can before the RRSP deadline.

Your income tax refund is usually in your hand in about ten business days (unless there is something on your return that CRA has concerns about) and you pay off the loan before that big bill arrives.

There are catch up loans available if you want to maximize the full amount stated on your assessment, from financial institutions, but unless you are really disciplined with your finances, I would not advise it.

So let's put that into figures for clarification.

Let us say that you have invested into your RRSP roughly $3,500.00 throughout the year.

You prepare your taxes a week before RRSP deadline; let us say that you will be getting back $6,000.00 on your income tax return.

You borrow say, $4,000.00.

You pay into your RRSP the $4,000.00; you have now invested $7,500.00 into your RRSP for the filing period allowed.

You now file your return, and get back $7,200.00 ($6000 that you were getting before hand + 30% of $4000 for a total of $7200 right?).

Then you pay off the RRSP loan before the first month is due. Now you really only have $3,200.00 instead of $6,000.00 left of your refund instead of what you were originally getting before the RRSP loan. But are you less off?

No! Why?

Because in essence you have an additional $4,000.00 in your RRSP's that you did not have before. So in actual fact you really have a personal gain (refund + RRSP) of $7,200.00 as opposed to the original $6,000.00 you were getting back before maximizing your RRSP, all in all using someone else's money, even if you can afford to put into it more money of your own, provided that your contribution ceiling for that year allows it.

RRIF's

Now! You have reached the age of 72 and Houston we have a problem.

All that money that you have spent years building up tax free into your RRSP's is now taxable if you take it out.

And it is a very sizable amount in due taxes too, not just a small percentage. What do we do!

Most of your fund managers will tell you to convert them into a RRIF (Registered Retirement Income Fund) and off course they are right.

However, by law, you have to withdraw approximately 3% of your total income, and that my friend is taxable.

But 3% is not as bad as having to pay tax on the total amount.

What can you do to protect yourself from getting taxed on that income?

Simple! Continue to work a part time home business in your spare time and for some retiree's there is no shortage of that.

Again, a network is easy, requires minimal effort and you don't need to commute.

All the expenses that you accumulate, while trying to generate an income should offset any tax liabilities on the little money you earn on your pensions and RIFF withdrawals.

Now if one has never contributed to an RRSP, or if one happens to be on disability, then one is really in dire straights.

The fact is that the government will not allow you to have assets of over $6,000.00 and earn no more than $160.00 of your income at the time of this writing.

What can you do? There is only one thing one can do. And that is, that you will have to be content on living with a monthly income of $964.00 a month for the rest of your days. So contributing to an RRSP early in life is an essential asset, unless one is born or inherits a handicap at a very early age.

That is really a trick and a half, since most decent apartments in any major city in North America rent for a bit over a thousand.

All I can say is unless you have a good pension from your ex employer, it is a challenge for the man and women who have contributed and paid his dues to this country to survive.

I got an e-mail the other day that I really do not know of its validity.

I tried to find some literature on it but could not. But I would like you guys to read it.

I suspect it to be true from those I have talked to and from the OAS slips of my clients, but without proof on the refugee end, I cannot say either way.

It goes as follows:

CANADA PENSION - A Must Read Only in Canada.

Do not apply for your old age pension...

Apply to be a refugee. It is interesting that the federal government provides a single refugee with a monthly allowance of $1,890.00 and each can get an additional $580.00 in social assistance for a total of $2,470.00.

This compares very well to a single pensioner who, after contributing to the growth and development of Canada for 40 or 50 years can only receive a monthly maximum of $1,012.00 in old age pension and Guaranteed Income Supplement.

Maybe our pensioners should apply as refugees!

Maybe we can get the refugees cut back to $1,012.00 and the pensioners up to $2,470.00, so they can enjoy the money they were forced to submit to the Canadian government for those 40 to 50 years.

If this is true my friends, guess who is footing the bill.

Donations

Most of us wander just how much credit do we get on our donations. Well here it is. On the first $200.00 we get a tax credit of 17% and 29% on anything over and above the $200.00 mark, to a maximum of 75% of our net income, except in Quebec, which is simply a non-refundable credit rate of 22%.

Once again this deduction can be pooled by both spouses, but regardless of who makes the claim, the tax savings is the same, and the great thing about this deduction however is that it can be carried over for the next 5 years.

If your donations is under a $1,000.00 though, you may want to consider carrying it over perhaps in the next two or three years to maximize your effectiveness, since you only receive 17% on the first $200.00

Receipts have to be issued by a registered Canadian charity, with a charity number printed on the receipt.

You see in the last few years all charities have to be registered, so that now CRA can and does dictate who one can donate to and who you cannot, if one is looking for a tax receipt for one's donation, which most people are. Leaving out small churches and charities, who do not qualify and there are many.

The guidelines are so stringent that many operate without the knowledge of CRA and rightfully so in my opinion. They do not want to issue all charities a number, so most figure why should they report to CRA their business and activities.

In my opinion, CRA needs to loosen up with churches and charities no matter on their size. If we all co-operate with each other then we all win.

Is there any wonder why so much dishonesty exists, especially when people are forced in doing so? That should never exist especially amongst Christians and other religious groups I am sure.

Even if a charity or church gets accepted there is still the burden of filling out a charity report annually and if one fails to do so, CRA will threaten that institution or church with a $500.00 fine and a permanent threat of cancellation of their charity number all together.

Further more, if a small church or individual with a registered ministry, does any kind of charity work and does not accept an income as in a case of three of my clients. CRA will not accept their deductions and expenses and occasionally go back up to 3 years, forcing them to pay back several tens of thousands of dollars.

Such as one of these three mentioned earlier in this book, whom go out every Saturday to feed the homeless in the streets of Toronto from their own personal income, without government or public help, and they are being asked to pay back almost $50,000.00 because they were denied their deductions for the last three years.

Whose responsibility is it to take care of these people anyway? Is it theirs? Or the government who will not help or take responsibility, and on top of that, are persecuting them for back taxes they figured they owe them.

If you live in Canada and work in the US, in which case you are allowed to claim up to 25% of your US income to a US charity in the same tax year. If you make your income in the US and bring it into Canada, then you may have to pay an additional 15% in excise tax.

Ins and outs of charity

Most of us donate money from the goodness of our hearts, as one should, especially if you are a member of a church, charity or if one truly cares for the less fortunate or cause that we are donating to.

But when you hear of a millionaire giving millions to a cause, do you really think that he or she is so generous as to give without getting back?

Perhaps some! Maybe, but who is kidding whom?

Here is how it works.

Just as a shirt costs $12.00 at Wal-Mart or any other retailer for example.

A huge retailer like Wal-Mart will buy these shirts in great quantities, perhaps by the thousands.

Let us assume that because of their huge buying power they purchase these shirts from the wholesaler for $2.00 or $3.00 lets say.

This may be a bit exaggerated, but we will roll with it for the purpose of simplicity of our example.

As a matter of fact with that kind of clout they are not offered that price, they dictate what price they want to pay for it and usually get it.

I have experienced that first hand when I worked in an electrical wholesaler in Toronto in my younger days.

Some of our bigger accounts would not ask us how much, they would tell us how much and if you could not meet their demand, they would buy from else where and usually got it.

But let us say that the fair market value of that shirt or in other words what the consumer is willing to pay for it is $12.00.

So twelve dollars it is. Simple enough, right?

Now let us say that a new wing in a hospital is to be built and thanks to the generous donation of Joe Millionaire, who has donated ten million dollars, this dream can now become a reality.

Just as Wal-Mart has the buying power derived from volume, so do the builders, by buying construction materials in volume at a dictate price.

So if a cinder block costs $5.00 each to a guy walking in off the street at Home Depot, it may cost the builders of this hospital $1.00 or less.

So what is happening here, Joe millionaire donates $10,000,000 enough to cover the cost of materials and labor for the finished product, but the hospital fund raisers will issue Joe millionaire a tax receipt for the Fair Market Value of that finished product which might be say $50,000,000.

This becomes a tax shelter for Joe millionaire and he gets back $14,500,000 of his donation in the form of a tax refund, if not more. Impressive wouldn't you say?

In a case such as a hospital or a museum let's say, Home Depot or any other store may also join in on the bandwagon and donate some of the material and get a tax receipt for the Fair Market Value as well on the material. Just as they do with Habitat for Humanity, at least in part.

They too, like Wal-mart, instead of buying a block for $1.00 they may buy it for .50 or .60 cents (as mentioned before, figures are exaggerated for the purpose of simplicity), but the charity is in their legal right to issue them a receipt for $5.00 which is the Fair Market value of that block.

I say, what works for Joe millionaire, may also apply to you and me.

There are legitimate charities out there, in which you can do this, but you might want to do your homework to see which ones are legitimate and which ones are not.

The last thing you need is a letter from CRA requesting you to pay it all back in the thousands, due to receipts that did not meet the Fair Market Value of the product donated.

Here is what CRA has to say regarding such illegitimate tax schemes.

Taxpayer alert

Warning: Participating in tax shelter gifting arrangements is likely to result in a tax bill!

Despite numerous warnings and audit actions by the Canada Revenue Agency (CRA), taxpayers are still participating in tax shelter gifting arrangements. The CRA is urging taxpayers to avoid these schemes.

The CRA is auditing all gifting arrangements

Taxpayers should be aware that the CRA plans to audit all tax shelter gifting arrangements. Every audit completed to date has resulted in a reassessment of tax, plus interest. In many cases the CRA has denied the "gift" completely. Penalties will be considered, especially where an investor was audited and reassessed for previously participating in a gifting arrangement.

Stats and Facts

- To date, the CRA has reassessed over 26,000 taxpayers who participated in these schemes, and denied about $1.4 billion in donations claimed.
- Audits of another 20,000 taxpayers involving $550 million in donation claims are just about complete.
- Audits on other arrangements involving over 50,000 taxpayers are about to begin.

Current Promotions

New schemes are being marketed that claim to be different from those for which the CRA has previously issued warnings. Taxpayers should avoid all schemes that promise donation receipts for 3 to 4 times the cash payment. It is the CRA's position that the proposed legislation, effective since 2003, will apply to reduce the donation credit to no more than the actual cash payment. Furthermore, as indicated above, completed audits have shown that there was effectively **no gift** being made in many cases, and as a result, the donation was reduced to zero.

Packages promoting these schemes sometimes include letters of commendation about the particular charity, which can give the impression of endorsing the scheme itself. These letters should not be interpreted as providing any assurance that these schemes do what they claim to be doing or that the promised tax benefits are in accordance with the *Income Tax Act*.

Get professional, independent advice

If you are still thinking about participating in a tax shelter gifting arrangement, it's very important that you get independent legal and tax advice. Independent advice means advice from a tax professional that is **not** connected to the scheme or promoter. If property is involved, you should also get independent advice on its true value. Packages from promoters will often claim to have legal or tax opinions from a law firm. You may find that these opinions contain very general comments and do not provide unconditional support for the scheme. Ask to see them, and have them reviewed by an independent professional.

In addition, participants who have been reassessed for previous participation in these schemes may also wish to obtain independent tax advice to determine their best options.

Tax shelter identification numbers

The CRA reminds taxpayers that tax shelter numbers are used for **identification purposes only**. These numbers identify both the schemes and those taxpayers who participate in them. They do not guarantee that taxpayers are entitled to receive the proposed tax benefits.

Not been contacted by the CRA yet?

The CRA generally has three years from the date of assessment to reassess taxpayers, and these audits can take over a year to complete. The fact that investors in these tax shelters have not been contacted and/or reassessed should not be interpreted as the CRA's acceptance of their claim.

There are a few that are scams, such as the donations of artwork. Since a Fair Market Value cannot be determined on an item that you bought from a garage sale or bazaar for a buck.

Rest assures that the government will make you pay it back, if you happen to get involved with any of them that are not legitimate.

This however is not the only way to obtain legitimate tax receipts from a charity.

You can also donate material things to a church, for example, food, clothing, cleaning supplies, quilts, décor and just about anything you like.

These are gifts in kind and by rights you are entitled to a tax receipt for the Fair Market Value of whatever you have donated.

Let me give you the CRA definition for gifts in kind.

Quote

"IT-297R2 Gifts in Kind to Charity and Others

NO: **IT-297R2**

DATE: March 21, 1990

SUBJECT: INCOME TAX ACT

Gifts in Kind to Charity and Others

REFERENCE: Subsections 118.1(1) and 110.1(1) (also sections 9, 13 and 39, subsections 110.6(3) and 118.1(3), and subparagraph 69(1) (b) (ii))

Application

This bulletin cancels and replaces Interpretation Bulletin IT-297R dated February 20, 1984. Vertical lines designate current revisions.

Summary

This bulletin discusses the tax consequences of making a gift in kind to charity or others and the valuation of that gift.

Discussion and Interpretation

1. A gift includes a gift in kind. The definition of a gift, the deducting provisions applicable to both individuals and corporations, and the requirements for official donation receipts are explained in the current version of IT-110 and the related Special Release.

2. The general rule in 4 below does not apply where the Act provides special rules for gifts in kind. These special rules are discussed in the current version of the following Interpretation Bulletins:

IT-244 - Gifts of Life Insurance Policies as Charitable Donations, IT-288 - Gifts of Capital Property to a Charity and Others, IT-407 - Disposition of Canadian Cultural Property, and IT-504 - Visual Artists and Writers.

3. Gifts in kind of a taxpayer include capital property, depreciable property, personal-use property including listed personal property (see the current version of IT-332), a leasehold interest, a residual interest (see the current version of IT-226), a right of any kind whatever, a license, a share, a chose in action **and inventory of a business**. A gift in kind, however, does not include a gift of services.

Where the property gifted was held jointly by a husband and wife, other than as partners in a partnership, whether the gift was made by the husband, wife or both parties, they may choose whichever allocation is most advantageous to them for the purpose of a claim by each of them under the deducting provisions. This discretionary allocation applies as well to subsequent year claims in respect of any unused portion of the donation. Such donation claims should be adequately explained upon filing of the applicable income tax returns, particularly in the case of the individual who uses a copy of the original receipt to support the claim.

4.   Generally, when anything is disposed of to any person by way of a gift inter vivos, **the taxpayer (donor) is deemed to have received proceeds of disposition equal to the fair market value of the property pursuant to subparagraph 69(1) (b) (ii).** Where the property was held jointly by a husband and wife, the proceeds of disposition must be allocated between them on the basis of the relative interest each spouse held in the property regardless of the discretionary allocation that may be made in respect of their claims under the deducting provisions as described in 3 above. Each taxpayer must therefore account for any
   (a) Income under section 9 if the property was inventory of a business, or
   (b) Capital gain or capital loss under section 39 if the property was a capital property, and
   (c) Recapture of capital cost allowance under section 13 if the property was depreciable property. It should be noted that although the gifts in kind discussed in the current versions of IT-288, IT-407 and IT-504 referred to in 2 above, are subject to special rules for the determination,

if any, of capital gains, any recapture of capital cost allowance with respect to such gifts of depreciable property is reported in the usual manner.

The fair market value of a gift in kind is also the relevant amount for the purposes of calculating the non-refundable and non-transferable federal tax credit under subsection 118.1(3) for individuals after 1987 and the deductible gift under subsection 110.1(1) for corporations after 1987, as well as the deductible gift under the legislation as it applied to all taxpayers prior to the 1988 taxation year.

5. If the taxpayer making the donation is an individual (other than a trust) and realizes a capital gain, the provisions of subsection 110.6(3) may apply. If the capital gains deduction has not been fully utilized, the individual may be able to fully or partially offset the capital gain referred to above with the subsection 110.6(3) deduction.

6. **The fair market value of a gift in kind as of the date of the donation (the date on which beneficial ownership is transferred from the donor to the donee) must be determined before an amount can be recorded on a receipt for tax purposes.** If the property was owned on Valuation Day (December 31, 1971), a valuation as of that date may also be required for capital gains purposes. The person who determines the fair market value of the property must be competent and qualified to evaluate the particular property being transferred by way of a gift. Property of little or only nominal value to the donor will not qualify as a gift in kind.

Used clothing of little value would be an example of a non-qualifying contribution.

7   Gifts to Her Majesty in right of Canada and Her Majesty in right of the provinces include gifts to an agent of the Crown. Whether a particular entity is an agent of the Crown in right of Canada or a province depends on whether the law creating the entity (a corporation, commission, gallery, etc.) expressly makes it an agent of the Crown or the entity is an agent of the Crown at common law.

8.   Section 118.1 and subsection 110.1(1) are not applicable to donations of property where its cost has been or should be charged as a business expense. For example, if a taxpayer transfers merchandise or supplies to a charity in consideration of a right, privilege, material benefit or advantage such as promotion or advertising for the taxpayer's business, then the transfer would not be a gift. For further information, see the current version of IT-110.

9.   A pamphlet entitled "Gifts in Kind", available at District Taxation Offices, provides a general discussion of this topic."

If you have a Network business and you happen to be the Pastor then you write off your purchases as part of your inventory, but you are also allowed to write what you have donated as a gift in kind to the church for the retail value of that merchandise.

As mentioned earlier, the church will have to issue a receipt for the donations to your business, provided that the church is registered as a charity with CRA.

Rental Income

Claiming your basement apartment

Some will try to hide claiming a basement apartment from CRA; reasoning is that, because they figure that, they will have to pay taxes on that rental income.

This is not only illegal, but a mistake as well.

With rental income you can also claim expenses that you could not have done so before.

For example; one may be charging a flat rate for a basement apartment, but a lot of expenses are shared, expenses such as utilities, maintenance, repairs, taxes, interest and so on.

Even some which are not shared such as part of your office.

Also if you have an adult son or daughter living with you, who are employed and is not paying rent, you can still charge them a minimal fee of $12.00 per year and still deduct the expenses anyway. As long as there is a designated rent, it is legitimate. What you charge for rent is your discretion.

In addition to the deductions mentioned, you may also claim depreciation on your house.

Even though that the person living in your house is a relative, sooner or later there will be repair that will need to be done.

Rental property outside your home

If you own property outside the home then you have some additional expenses that you would normally do not renting your basement apartment.

Such a small part of your vehicle expenses.

You may have an office at the building and drive there on a daily basis.

Your telephone, instead of having someone coming up from the basement and telling you that they need this or that repaired, now you have tenants calling you.

You may have problems with one or more tenants and have tribunal costs, interest on the property, taxes and so on.

So, when you have one or more units outside your place of residence, all of a sudden you have a variety of additional expenses you did not have before.

Again you can take advantage of the tax benefits from buying supplies from the network and selling them to the building for its maintenance and up keep.

Child Care

Is claiming babysitting income a bad thing?

Again a lot of people try to hide babysitting income because they figure that they will be taxed on that as additional income.

And again, that is illegal and a mistake.

Looking after a child or many children is a business of its own, and if you run it from your home, there are many expenses involved, just as any other home business.

Home businesses do not have to be registered provided that it is run under your personal name.

As a part time business, you are entitled to write off the same expenses as anyone else.

From the parent's side of the coin, it also benefits you, since babysitters are deductible along side summer camps, fitness programs, boarding schools and after school programs.

Provided that these expenses come as a result, that enables you to earn an income.

The lower income earner generally deducts these expenses, although there are some exceptions, especially in the province of Quebec.

For example, if the lower income individual is attending school or occupational training.

One is allowed to claim 75% for low income families and as low as 26% for higher income families up to $7,000.00 for each child under the age of seven and $4000.00 for each child over the age of seven but under 16. Except in Quebec those figures are $5,000.00 and $3,000.00 in that order.

As of year 2000, one can deduct up to $10,000.00 in deductions for children with disabilities.

However at a federal level this deduction is limited to only two thirds of ones income and it does not apply in Quebec.

Moving Expenses

You may qualify for a moving expense if you move anywhere in Canada, to be at least 40 Km closer to a place of employment or educational institution.

This deduction only applies for reasons of earning an income or to acquire an education full time in a post secondary institution for the purpose of earning an income, even if the job is only on a part time basis.

This deduction does not apply for the purpose of retiring unless you are still working part time during retirement or have a consulting income.

Bellow is a list of expenses that can be deducted:

- Hiring Movers
- Truck or Van rentals, if you are moving on your own.
- Storage
- Meals and Lodging on route for you and the family
- Costs involved in changing the address on documentation, utilities or mail
- The cost of terminating or breaking a lease
- The cost of selling your home such as, Legal fees and Real Estate commissions
- Mortgage interest and Property tax up to $5,000.00 as well as maintenance on the previous residence

These deductions apply to anyone including students moving away to take on summer employment, on a co-op program, start a business or take on full time employment.

If deductions do not warrant a high enough income for that year to make a difference, this deduction can be carried forward to a following year, but no more than one year.

Medical Expenses

One may claim medical expenses if they are more than 3% of their net income or $1884.00 which ever is less at the time this book was written.

Married couples and Common Law partner may combine their claims as long as the income from the spouse with the lower income is taxable.

In Quebec however it is just simply 3% of expenses in excess of your total family income.

That is to say, the total family income in Quebec is the family's total net income minus (RPP) registered pension plan and RRSP contributions for both spouses.

This way of calculating a net income greatly reduces the tax benefit for medical expenses in that province.

For Federal and Quebec income tax purposes, as of 1997 and subsequent years, persons earning at least $2,500.00 are eligible for a refundable tax credit, known as The Refundable Medical Expense Tax Credit.

The credit is limited to $500.00 or 25% of the allowable expenses (which is ever is less) and it is reduced by 5% if the family net income exceeds $16,069.00.

If both spouses claim their medical expenses individually on their return, then they both may be entitled to this credit.

You may also claim any medical expense you may have incurred for a relative living with you and is a Canadian resident during that filing year.

Medical claims aside from your spouse will be reduced by four times the amount of that relative's net income if it exceeds the basic amount of $8,377.00. In Quebec this figure is 2.9 times the net income.

Premiums paid to a plan, such as Blue Cross, Green Shield or an employer plan, are tax deductible, even if it only covers you while you are on vacation.

You do not have to file your medical in the year that you receive them. CRA allows you to file any 12-month period in the year in which you are filing.

The medical receipts that one is allowed to file is not restricted to prescriptions, they may also include orthopedics, hearing aids and batteries, nursing or retirement homes, but not items like aspirin, vitamins or supplements.

These may be claimed as inventory in your home business for the purpose of resale but not in the medical section of your return.

Chapter 5

Other Credits and Deductions

Equivalent-to-spouse amount

The equivalent to spouse amount, which most of us are aware and which in the year that this book was written (2007) was $7,824.00, for a spouse who's income is less than $615.00.

But did you also know that this credit also applies to a single, separated or divorced person, who supports a family member with a net income of less than $8,377.00 (Basic Personal Amount)?

This family member can be your kids, mother, brother etc.

However, if it is your children then they must be under 18, unless the child has some form of handicap, that is to say a mental or physical infirmity.

Here is a list of a few other deductions not previously mentioned. Some are too obvious to warrant an explanation.

Almost all those with explanations are quoted right from the CRA tax benefit guide.

- Union Dues
- Disability Support deduction
- Business Investment loss
- Support Payments - Most child support payments paid according to a written agreement or court order dated after April 1997, are not deductible.
- Carrying charges and interest expenses - You can claim the following carrying charges and interest you paid to earn income from investments. Such as;
    - o Fees paid to rent a safety deposit box.
    - o Interest paid for the purchase of Canada Savings Bonds through payroll deductions.
    - o Investment loans
    - o In some cases financial planning and Investment counseling fees, such as investment advice or for recording investment income.
    - o Fees to manage or take care of your investments (other than administration fees you paid for your registered retirement savings plan or registered retirement income fund), including safety deposit box charges.
    - o Fees to have someone complete your return, but only if you have income from a business or property, accounting is a usual part of the operations of your business or property, and you did not use the amounts claimed to reduce the business or property income you reported; and most interest you pay on money you borrow for

investment purposes, but generally only as long as you use it to try to earn investment income, including interest and dividends. However, if the only earnings your investment can produce are capital gains, you cannot claim the interest you paid.

- Dividend Income – Dividend income is transferable from one spouse to another. By doing this, it will increase a spouse credit for that person and it must originate from a Canadian corporation
- Deductions for CPP or QPP contributions on self employment - You can claim, on this line, **half** of the total of your Canada Pension Plan (CPP) or Quebec Pension Plan (QPP) contributions, if any, **from Schedule 8.** You also can claim, on line 310 on Schedule 1, an amount **for the other half.** You can claim contributions you:

  1. Have to make on self-employment and limited or non-active partnership income;
  2. Choose to make on certain employment income (see "Making additional CPP contributions" at line 308); and
  3. Choose to make on your provincial income tax return for Quebec on certain employment income (see your Quebec provincial guide).

The amount of CPP or QPP contributions that you have to make, or choose to make, will depend on how much you have already contributed to the CPP or QPP as an employee, as shown in boxes 16 and 17 of your T4 slips.

- **Clergy** – One can claim this if one is a member of the clergy and takes up permanent residence in a church property.
- **Employee relocation loan deduction**

Credits from Schedule 1

- **Public transit passes**
- **Adoption expenses** - You can claim a credit for eligible adoption expenses related to the adoption of a child who is under 18. The **maximum claim** for each child is $10,220.

    The claim for eligible expenses may be split between two adoptive parents as long as the combined total claim is not more than the amount before the split.

    Parents can claim these incurred expenses in the tax year that includes the end of the adoption period in respect of the child. The adoption period:

    1. Begins at the earlier of the time that the eligible child's adoption file is opened with a provincial or territorial ministry responsible for adoption (or with an adoption agency licensed by a provincial or territorial government) and the time, if any, that an application related to the adoption is made to a Canadian court; and
    2. Ends at the later of the time an adoption order is issued by, or recognized by, a government in Canada in respect of that child, and the time

that the child first begins to reside permanently with you.

- **Pension income amounts** - Previously, you were able to claim a credit on the first $1,000 of eligible pension or annuity income reported on line 115 or line 129 of your return. Under proposed legislation, the maximum amount of eligible pension income that can be used to calculate the credit is increased to $2,000.

  You may be able to transfer all or part of your pension income amount to your spouse or common-law partner or to claim all or part of his or her pension income amount

- **Caregiver** amount - If, at any time in *2006*, you (either alone or with another person) maintained a dwelling where you and a dependant lived, you may be able to claim a maximum amount of $3,933. The dependant must have been one of the following individuals:

  1. Your or your spouse or common-law partner's child or grandchild; or
  2. Your or your spouse or common-law partner's brother, sister, niece, nephew, aunt, uncle, parent, or grandparent who was resident in Canada. You cannot claim this amount for a person who was only visiting you.

In addition, you can claim an amount for more than one dependant as long as each one meets **all** of the following conditions. The person must have:

1. Been 18 or over at the time he or she lived with you;
2. Had a net income (line 236 of his or her return, or what line 236 would be if he or she filed a return) of less than $17,363; and
3. Been dependent on you due to mental or physical infirmity or, if he or she is your or your spouse or common-law partner's parent or grandparent, born in *1941* or earlier.

If you were required to make support payments for a child, you cannot claim an amount on line 315 for that child. However, if you were separated from your spouse or common-law partner for only **part of 2006** due to a breakdown in your relationship, you can still claim an amount for that child on line 315 (plus any allowable amounts on lines 305 and 318) as long as you do not claim any support amounts paid to your spouse or common-law partner on line 220, You may claim whichever is better for you.

*   **Disability amount** - To claim this amount, you must have a severe and prolonged impairment in physical or mental functions during *2006*. Impairment is prolonged if it has lasted, or is expected to last, for a continuous period of at least 12 months. You can claim $6,741 if a qualified practitioner certifies that one of the following conditions applies:

    A. You are **blind**, even with the use of corrective lenses or medication.
    B. You are **markedly restricted** in a basic activity of daily living. Markedly restricted means that all or substantially all the time, you are unable, or it takes you an inordinate amount of time, to do

at least one of the basic activities of daily living, even with therapy (other than life-sustaining therapy, see condition C), the use of appropriate devices, and medication. The **basic activities of daily living** are speaking, hearing, walking, elimination (bowel or bladder functions), feeding (which does not include preparing food due to dietary restrictions, or obtaining food), dressing (which does not include obtaining clothing), and mental functions necessary for everyday life.

C. You require **life-sustaining therapy** to support a vital function, such as clapping therapy to help in breathing or kidney dialysis to filter your blood. This therapy must have been required at least 3 times per week at an average of at least 14 total hours per week. Time spent on therapy must be time that is dedicated to the therapy, and takes you away from normal everyday activities.

D. Qualifying therapy does not include activities such as following a dietary restriction or regime, exercising, traveling to receive the therapy, attending medical appointments (other than appointments where the therapy is received), shopping for medication, or recuperating after therapy.

E. Where the therapy has been determined to require a regular dosage of medication that needs to be adjusted on a daily basis, the activities directly involved in determining the appropriate dosage are considered part of the therapy.

F. In the case of a child who is unable to perform the activities related to the therapy as a result of his or her age, the time spent by the child's primary caregivers performing and supervising these activities is time dedicated to the therapy. For example, children who require insulin therapy to treat Type 1 diabetes and who cannot independently adjust the insulin dosage may now qualify (for 2005 and subsequent years only).

G. You do not meet the criteria in B, but your ability to perform more than one basic activity of daily living is significantly restricted, and the cumulative effect of your restrictions is equivalent to a marked restriction (see definition in B) in one basic activity of daily living. The significant restrictions must be present together, all or substantially all the time. Vision may be included in combination with the basic activities of daily living.

- **Disability amount transferred from a dependent** - You may be able to claim all or part of your dependant's disability amount (line 316) if he or she was resident in Canada at any time in *2006* and was dependent on you for all or some of the basic necessities of life (food, shelter, or clothing).

In addition, **one** of the following situations has to apply:

- You claimed an amount on line 305 for that dependant, or you could have if you did not have a spouse or common-law partner and if the dependant did not have any income.
- The dependant was your or your spouse or common-law partner's parent, grandparent, child, grandchild, brother, sister, aunt, uncle, niece, or nephew, and you claimed an amount on <u>line 306</u> or <u>315</u> for that dependant, or you could have if he or she had no income and had been 18 years of age or older in *2006*.

If you are required to make support payments for your child, you **cannot** claim a transfer of that child's disability amount. However, if you were separated from your spouse or common-law partner for only **part of *2006*** due to a breakdown in your relationship, you can still claim an amount for that child on line 318 (plus any allowable amounts on lines 305, 306, and 315) as long as you do not claim any support amounts paid to your spouse or common-law partner on line 220. You may claim whichever is better for you.

Notes

You **cannot** claim this credit if the spouse or common-law partner of the person with a disability is already claiming the disability amount or any other non-refundable tax credit (other than medical expenses) for the person with a disability.

If you are splitting this claim with another individual, attach a note to your paper return including the name and social insurance number of the other individual who is making this claim. The total claimed for that dependant couldn't be more than the maximum amount allowed for that dependant.

If you or anyone else paid for an attendant, or for care in an establishment, special rules may apply

- **Interest paid on student loans**
- **Tuition, education and text book amounts**
- **Tuition, education and text book amounts transferred from a child**
- **Amounts transferred from your spouse or common law partner** - You may be able to claim all or part of the following amounts for which your spouse or common-law partner qualifies: for *2006* that your spouse or common-law partner designates. The maximum amount that your spouse or common-law partner can transfer is $5,000 minus the amounts that he or she uses, even if there is still an unused part.

Note

Your spouse or common-law partner cannot transfer to you any tuition, education, and textbook amounts carried forward from a previous year. In addition, he or she cannot transfer any unused amounts to you if you were separated because of a breakdown in your relationship for a period of 90 days or more that included December 31, *2006*.

- The **age amount** (line 301) if your spouse or common-law partner was 65 or older;

- The **pension income amount** – Anyone receiving an employer pension plan, is entitled to claim up to $1000.00 per year. I which creates a $170.00 in tax credits.

If you are over 65 and you are receiving income from an RRSP or a RRIF, this credit will also apply on the first $1000.00 of income, tax-free. This may also be transferable to your spouse if, for whatever reason you are not able to claim it yourself.

In Quebec it varies a bit and this amount is determined by the families net income minus RRSP and RPP contributions, I believe to be a single deduction of 15% of an amount by which the net family income exceeds %26,000.00 and shared between the spouses as they see fit.

- The **disability tax credit** – This is a non-refundable credit of $4,293.00 with prolonged physical or mental infirmity such as Alzheimer's. This credit was designed to provide tax assistance to tax payer's providing in home assistance for the elderly born in 1935 or earlier or a child whose income is less than $14,047.00 and reduce his or her federal tax up to $400.00. But in order to qualify for this credit, the tax payer's doctor must certify it. Also, as of the year 2000 a child under 18, who qualifies for the disability amount, can pick up an additional amount of $2,941.00. However this claim is reduced if child care and attendant care exceeds $2000.00
- **Federal Tax On Split Income** - Certain income of a child who was born in *1989* or later is treated differently from other types of income. It is subject to a special tax, but also qualifies for a deduction.

There are other tax credits that are quite specific to certain industries such as research and development, overseas employment tax credits.... But for the common foe, such as you and I, need not to get into all of it.

What we are mostly concerned with is common deductions that the majority of us encounter, while preparing our taxes.

So I believe that for the most part we have our credits and deductions covered as explained by CRA's tax and benefit guide.

Conclusion

Deferring

Just as the secret to success is to Delegate, Delegate and Delegate, the secret to good tax planning is Defer, Defer and Defer.

The most prominent way of deferring taxes is of course RRSP's. If you do not have a portfolio, you may want to consider starting one as soon as possible.

Depending on your contribution ceiling which is determined by tax bracket, usually stated at the bottom of your previous year's assessment, RRSP's are tax deductible and the income tax free until one's attempt to cash them.

The secret is not to cash them as discusses earlier in Chapter 4.

There are literary dozens more deductions more that we could get into, such as the employee GST rebate tax deductions.

One can deduct personal expenses, while working for someone else, when one is asked to pay for such things from their own pocket such as meals, lodging, car expenses, etc., Apprentice tools deductions, musician tax credits or special tax credits for the movie industry.

We could go on and on and on, but I believe that what we have covered enough ground in this book, to make it sufficient for the common working person to maximize their return and keep their money where it belongs.

In your pocket!

Should you have any questions or need information regarding this book or your particular situation, feel free to call me at 416-619-7578 during business hours.

References

- MSN Money
- CRA web site
- Articles and e-mails sent to me by friends and relatives
- The internet
- The Income Tax Act
- The Canadian Financial Securities Program – By Mike Murphy
- Political Cartoons - Michael's Journal

www.ingramcontent.com/pod-product-compliance
Lightning Source LLC
Chambersburg PA
CBHW022023170526
45157CB00003B/1335